CHE

CHE

A REVOLUTIONARY ICON

LUIS ENRIQUE MARTINEZ

CHARTWELL
BOOKS

CHE GUEVARA
(1928 – 1967)
Ernesto "Che" Guevara de la Serna,
theoretician and tactician of guerrilla warfare,
prominent figure in the Cuban Revolution,
and guerrilla leader in South America.

CONTENTS

INTRODUCTION

What are we to make of Che Guevara? A man whose image is omnipresent in modern culture, either in the form of the famous photograph taken of him by Alberto Korda, or in stylistic suggestions that can be found everywhere from a Madonna album cover to a bold red star on a T-shirt. Who was this icon who lived the most fantastic of lives, who brought change to a nation not his own, and longed to spread change across the world?

He was certainly a walking contradiction. An educated, cultured man, with a wonderful sense of humor, he wrote poetry and grew up in a middle-class family. Yet he had no compunction about committing violence to achieve his aims.

In the Sierra Maestra in Cuba, he was the first to volunteer to put a bullet in the head of a traitor, and wholeheartedly advocated violent revolution not only in Cuba but in Africa and South America. He described himself in his last letter to his wife Aleida March, as he prepared to instigate revolution in Bolivia:

> *I'm a combination of adventurer and bourgeois, with a terrible yearning to come home, while at the same time, anxious to realize my dreams.*

Despite his enigmatic split personality, or maybe because of it, we seem unable to resist the temptation to view him as a romantic figure. We are unable to see beyond the twinkling eyes and beard, the beret with the star, and the Cuban cigar. But there definitely was a romantic side to this perplexing character. His travels in Latin and Central America before he blossomed into a revolutionary testify to that.

The Motorcycle Diaries, his book documenting his 1952 journey with his friend Alberto Granado, has helped turn him into not only a revolutionary but also a kind of Latin American Jack Kerouac. The 2004 film of the book starring Mexican actor Gael García Bernal further reinforced the romantic perception of the iconic guerrilla commander.

Che was also a serious politician, and the principal theorist behind the Cuban Revolution as well as a proud fighter for

Che Guevara as diplomat and international statesman, 1964.

it. His idea of the New Man, a person who worked for the satisfaction of serving his community or his nation, was something he never deviated from. Society would look after such a man and society would benefit from his efforts.

He practiced what he preached. He spent every Sunday when he was a minister in the Cuban government working on sugar-cane plantations, and when times were hard because of the American blockade, he lived on the same rations as every other Cuban citizen.

When he left his wife and family to travel to Bolivia toward the end of his life, he was proud of the fact that he left them nothing, knowing that Fidel Castro and the state would take care of them. It was the type of thinking that put him at odds with the politicians of the Soviet Union who had formed a new type of elite, enjoying privilege and luxuries that the ordinary people could never aspire to.

Perhaps above all else, we should admire Che Guevara for his unwavering bravery. He had the courage of his convictions, and he was prepared to die for them. Even in Bolivia when he was sick, suffering from asthma, and seeing his whole operation falling apart, he led by example. His good friend Harry Villegas highlighted Che's strength of character in his diary:

It was the type of courage that permitted him to face death stoically, knowing that he had given everything he had for his idea of a better world.

Yet he remains a total conundrum. A Marxist Communist revolutionary whose image is now used to sell all kinds of capitalist merchandise across the globe. It would have been Che's worst nightmare. As his associate Ciro Bustos said, if Che came back and saw it, he would believe he had failed.

This book tells the story of the astonishing individual who was Che Guevara, a man of extreme contrasts—part truth, part fantasy—who was both inspiring and horrifying in equal measure.

Fidel Castro (left) lights his cigar while Che Guevara looks on in the early days of their guerrilla campaign in the Sierra Maestra mountains, Cuba, 1956.

PART ONE

THE BLOOD OF IRISH REBELS

IN MY SON'S VEINS FLOWED
THE BLOOD OF IRISH REBELS.

ERNESTO GUEVARA LYNCH,
CHE GUEVARA'S FATHER

CHAPTER 1

THE ROOTS OF REBELLION

The baby who became the revolutionary Che Guevara was born prematurely on June 14, 1928, in Rosario, the largest city in the north-eastern Argentinean province of Santa Fe. There are suggestions, however, that he was actually born on May 14, and that his mother had already been pregnant when she married her husband. The date on the birth certificate may have been falsified to save her from scandal.

IN PUERTO CARAGUATAY

Whatever his birth date, his parents Ernesto Guevara Lynch and Celia de la Serna y Llosa, followed Argentinean tradition by calling their first-born son Ernesto after his father, but he would always be known as Ernestito by his family.

He was born shortly after the couple arrived in the bustling town of Rosario, the heavily pregnant Celia having made the arduous journey with her husband down the Paraná River from their *yerba mate* plantation in Puerto Caraguatay in the area of Misiones in the north-eastern corner of Argentina. Ernesto Sr. had decided to start a business milling *mate*, grinding it to the fine leaf needed to make the beverage, and thought Rosario, a thriving industrial town, would be a good location.

They soon returned to Puerto Caraguatay where they lived in a house—known as "*la calesita*" (the "merry-go-round") because of its design—built by Ernesto Sr. who was a master builder. It was a small town and not unpleasant, but Ernesto Sr. thought the area was becoming a little dangerous because of its high incidence of crime. It was also true, however, that growing *mate* was proving difficult for him and profits were dwindling.

Ernesto Guevara at age 1 in 1929 (left) and growing up as a boy in Argentina in 1934 at age 6 (right).

THE GUEVARA FAMILY ORIGINS

• • • • • • • • • • •

A large number of the Argentinean families who fought for independence from Spain originated in the Basque region of northern Spain and, indeed, Guevara is a Basque surname.

The Guevara family were of Spanish and Irish origins and were not, as some have claimed, upper-class. Certainly, they were privileged but not aristocrats, especially as the Argentinean constitution, put together in 1813 when the country freed itself from Spanish hegemony, expressly forbid such social divisions, declaring all men to be equal.

By the 1840s Argentina was ruled by a *caudillo*, or dictator—the first of many. Juan Manuel de Rosas (1793 – 1877) was a tyrant who imprisoned or exiled his opponents. One family that fell victim to his repression was the Lynches. Patricio Lynch had arrived in Buenos Aires from Galway, Ireland, in the eighteenth century and married into the city's elite.

By the time Rosas came to power, the Lynches were one of the country's leading land-owning families. But in 1840 their land and possessions were seized by Rosas' followers, and Che's great-great-grandfather, Colonel Francisco Lynch y Arandia was murdered after expressing opposition to Rosas. Fortunately, his son Francisco was able to flee to Chile.

Around the same time, the brothers Juan Antonio and José Gabriel Guevara were also forced into exile in Chile, having had their properties expropriated. Both families were part of a movement to remove Rosas from power, relocating to the coastal town of Valparaiso along with a number of other opponents to the Argentinean dictator.

In January 1848, the discovery of gold in California gave the exiles an opportunity to get rich. The Guevaras and Lynches formed a company with another exile, José Carreas, and, having purchased a two-masted ship, set sail for California. They arrived in San Francisco where the Guevaras bought equipment, and in the winter of 1848 began searching for gold in the Sacramento River valley. It was to no avail, however, and they were forced to return to San Francisco after a year.

In 1852 the dictator Rosas, having been in power for over twenty years, was finally overthrown. The exiles could return to their homeland where they hoped they could repossess the properties that had been stolen from them.

Juan Antonio Guevara had by this time married Concepcíon, and they had a son whom they named Roberto. Eager to bring their son up as an Argentinean, the Guevaras returned home, leaving Francisco Lynch in California. They regained their land in Mendoza and Juan Antonio's son, Roberto Guevara Castro, was granted Argentinean citizenship.

Francisco Lynch in the meantime, had become wealthy, had married, and had a daughter Ana. But Francisco was homesick, and eventually decided to return to Argentina. Soon, Roberto Guevara, now 26, was courting Ana Lynch, and after they married, she gave birth to Ernesto Guevara Lynch, the father of Che Guevara.

A teenage Ernesto (left) with his parents and siblings, 1944. Seated beside him from left to right: Celia (mother), Celia (sister), Roberto, Juan Martín, Ernesto (father) and Ana María.

The birth of Ernestito provided him with an excuse to put the plantation up for sale and move on.

The child, it transpired, suffered from asthma, something that would be a blight on his entire life, although he always faced the discomfort and, indeed, the life-threatening problems it dealt him, with remarkable stoicism.

HARD TIMES IN ALTA GRACIA

The *mate* plantation was not at all what Ernesto Sr. had expected and he was certainly not a businessman of the caliber of his grandfather Francisco Lynch. He was provided with an excuse to bring his farming career to an end on May 2, 1930. On that day, his son, not yet two years old, suffered his first asthma attack and thereafter the attacks occurred at regular intervals.

His parents began to fear for the boy's life as he struggled to breathe. Every treatment they tried failed until the doctor recommended that the only way to deal with the child's condition was to move to an environment that provided clear, dry air. They relocated to Alta Gracia in the mountains of the province of Córdoba in the center of the country.

They moved into a good part of town, but their house, Villa Nydia, on Calle Chile, was slightly shabby and they had little money, Ernestito's treatments and the failure of the *mate* farm having depleted their resources. Furthermore, Ernesto Sr. found it hard to find work. He had never completed his architectural training and had little experience in any field of work apart from growing *mate*. Realizing that his architectural training could prove useful in construction work, he became a builder.

MARRIAGE BREAKDOWN

In Alta Gracia, the Guevaras had four more children—Celia, Roberto, Ana María, and Juan Martín. Celia always felt tremendous guilt because of her eldest son's asthma. The day of his first attack, she had taken him swimming in bad weather. Ernesto Sr. later described the day:

> It was freezing cold and there was a southeaster. Celia was an excellent swimmer and the weather did not bother her. She had gone to swim at the Nautico San Isidro near the house where we lived. The second of May I had gone to look for her in the afternoon. She was very young and somewhat thoughtless. She did not think for a moment that the weather might harm the child. When we left the club, Ernesto was in very bad condition. We went to the office of an old physician—I do not remember his name—who was a neighbor of ours. It was then that we learned of Ernesto's ailment.

His asthma attacks were so frequent that he was unable to go to primary school, and Celia had to tutor him at home. The attacks were so bad that very often Ernesto Sr. would sit by his son's bedside all night, leaving him exhausted in the morning. Every cough, meanwhile, was another nail in Celia's heart. It undoubtedly contributed to the increasing alienation of Ernesto Sr. and Celia, a distance that eventually led to their separation.

DEVELOPING AN IDEOLOGY

Ernestito's asthma also created problems with his siblings because he was undoubtedly Celia's favorite. His younger brothers and sisters often turned on him, tormenting him and even physically attacking him. He fought back, but the odds of three against one were usually too great. Celia taught him French and he learned about French culture and literature. He proved to be good at learning languages.

Thus, his mother became the dominant influence in his young life and the ideas of politics, Argentina, and life in general that he began to develop were essentially hers. His father did not play nearly so great a role in his development, his relationship with his children was far more easy-going than Celia's and he

CELIA DE LA SERNA

Celia de la Serna (1906 – 65), Che's mother, was two years younger than Che's father, Ernesto Guevara Lynch. Her background, like his, was patrician, and her wealthy and hugely respected family had Spanish aristocrats among its ancestors. It also had grand connections in the New World, including a family member who had been Viceroy of Upper Peru, and fought against the great Latin American independence leaders, Simón Bolívar (1783 – 1830) and José de San Martín (1778 – 1850).

Not long after the end of World War I, Celia's parents died within a short time of one another. Of a rebellious nature and stubborn but with a sharp intelligence, she was just what the easy-going Ernesto Guevara Lynch needed, someone to push him into action.

A good-looking young woman, she had been pursued by the young upper-class men of Buenos Aires but was disdainful of their arrogance and conservative ways. She was anything but conservative, and scandalized people with her views and the way she lived. She cut her hair short, drove a car, and signed her own checks.

She probably sensed that Ernesto was like her deep down inside, and the two got married. At the time, he was a student of architecture but was bored and she was similarly bored with life in Buenos Aires. Celia owned—in partnership with her eleven siblings—a parcel of land in Misiones, and she and her new husband decided to move there.

Celia was the most profound intellectual influence on her eldest son Che Guevara until he met Fidel Castro in 1955. A life-long militant communist, she raised five children virtually on her own after Ernesto left her following numerous affairs and many ferocious arguments. Celia died in Buenos Aires in 1967 after fighting cancer for over twenty years. Che was devastated when he learned of his mother's death while he was in Africa inciting revolution in the Congo.

was more of a friend to them than anything else. He certainly shared Celia's philosophy and ideology but his views were less extreme.

The young Ernestito thus developed his hatred of the elite upper-classes, the bourgeoisie, and the prevailing political, economic, and social system. He and his siblings were inculcated with his parents' political principles. It was not a house in which political debate was encouraged, and no one was permitted to have an alternative opinion.

Nonetheless, the house in Alta Gracia hosted many different children as the Guevaras encouraged their family to bring home whomever they wanted. One of Ernestito's friends described what it was like in those days:

> *The Guevaras kept their house wide open to everybody and this delighted the neighborhood children. In fact, they encouraged their own children to be as democratic as possible and to bring everyone they wished for a visit. Workers, mechanics, caddies, newsboys, people from all walks of life would meet to socialize with the Guevaras' upper-class friends.*

Ernesto Guevara at age 12 in 1940.

A NATURAL LEADER

Ernestito's father described him as a timid child, but "never introverted nor reserved," adding:

> *… ever since he was a lad he had the soul of a leader. At the age of six he was the leader of all the children in the neighborhood. All came to my house … All came with him. And he captained them.*

This is a view endorsed by Ernestito's childhood friend, Dolores Moyano Martín:

> *As a child, Ernesto was a natural leader. Ernesto, then about seven or eight years old, was the leader of a gang of kids, golf-course caddies and the sons of peons who worked in the nearby hills. He would often challenge the children of the local gentility and sons of well-to-do families vacationing in Alta Gracia to a soccer match. Ernesto's proletarian team would win decisively, and the losers would go home weeping to mama, with Ernesto and his gang taunting them.*

Not everyone agreed with this version of Ernesto as a boy. One school friend asserts that he was a "very sweet and reserved boy." He adds that he was "a serious youth, too much so for his age, prematurely mature."

One biographer describes him as "rather sullen, very silent, introverted." The reality is that Ernesto was a complicated child who could be out in front of the crowd, but who could also shun public display, quiet in a crowd of people, and seemingly reserved and withdrawn. It is no less than the type of man he grew up to be.

Ernesto was merely an average student, seemingly bored with academic routine, and with no great pass rate in exams. This is not to denigrate his intellectual capacity, however, as he read a wide range of books, both Argentinean and foreign. As his father said:

> *He read everything. He started, of course, with Salgari. Then he read Verne. Adventure stories aroused him. He started to read political works also when he was small … in my house we had an abundant library that included all subjects … Marx and Engels, and many other writers.*

THE SPANISH CIVIL WAR

• • • • • • • • • •

The Spanish Civil War was fought from July 1936 until April 1939 between the Republicans who supported the democratic leftist Second Spanish Republic government, and the Nationalists, a conservative group led by General Francisco Franco (1892 – 1975).

It began after an unsuccessful coup against the Second Republic by forces led by General Emilio Mola (1887 – 1937) who was known as "El Director." General Franco, at the time the head of an army on the Canary Islands, received support from Nazi Germany and Fascist Italy in getting his troops transported rapidly to Andalucia where he became the head of the Nationalists.

Support came from military forces from Morocco—at the time a Spanish protectorate— Pamplona, Burgos, Zaragoza, Valladolid, Cádiz, Córdoba, and Seville, but the cities of Madrid, Barcelona, Valencia, Bilbao, and Málaga remained government strongholds while the Nationalists and the Republicans fought for power.

The Nationalists were supported militarily by Hitler's Germany, Mussolini's Italy, and Portugal, while the Republicans (also known as Loyalists) were supported by the Soviet Union and Mexico, at the time a leftist state. France, the United Kingdom, and other countries adopted a policy of neutrality but around 40,000 non-Spaniards, representing fifty-three nations, joined what were known as the International Brigades.

In 1937 the Nationalists advanced northward and captured most of Spain's northern coastline. Madrid was besieged throughout the war and much of Catalonia was taken in 1938. In 1939 the conflict ended in victory for the Nationalists, leading to thousands of Spaniards who sympathized with the Republicans fleeing the country.

Many went to refugee camps in southern France and those who remained in Spain were subjected to persecution by the Nationalists. Franco established a dictatorship and ruled for thirty-six years, from 1939 until his death in 1975.

Street fighting in the Basque town of Irun during the Spanish Civil War, 1936.

POLITICAL TURMOIL IN ARGENTINA

• • • • • • • • • •

The first eighteen years of Ernesto Guevara's life were marked by political turmoil in his home country. Argentina staggered from one political crisis to another between 1930 and 1946. From 1916 until 1930, the centrist, social-liberal Radical Civic Union was in power and a measure of democracy had prevailed. The Radicals championed universal male suffrage and promised to tackle Argentina's social problems and eradicate poverty.

In 1930, the corrupt government of the aging president Hipolito Yrigoyen (1852 – 1933) was deposed in a military coup led by general José Félix Uriburu (1868 – 1932) and for the next thirteen years, conservative military governments ruled the country, supported by the banks, business, and the Church. Elections were manipulated and opponents were ruthlessly eliminated.

The rise of Fascism and Nazism in Europe had a huge effect on Argentina, many of whose officers had been the recipients of military training in Italy and Germany. Thus, when he came to power, Uriburu advocated a Fascist state and tried to abolish the Argentinean Congress.

General Augustin P. Justo (1876 – 1943) followed Uriburu, but although his dictatorship was more benign, opposition was still not tolerated and electoral fraud was rife. He permitted foreign control of Argentinean interests, the British, for instance, retaining control of the inefficient and badly-run Argentinean railway system. Anti-foreign sentiment erupted during this period.

Wealthy lawyer and socialite Roberto M. Ortiz (1886 – 1942) was selected by Justo as his successor. His election was a disgraceful example of electoral fraud but, to his credit—and everyone's surprise—he tried to reimpose honest elections and supported the Allies against the Axis powers in World War II.

Ortiz was forced out of office by ill health and replaced by his vice president, Ramón S. Castillo (1873 – 1944) who brought a return to the old corrupt ways. Castillo supported the Axis powers, and Argentina was the only country that refused to break with the Axis powers at the Rio de Janeiro conference of American Foreign Ministers in 1942.

Elections were to be held in 1943 but Castillo's reputation for election fraud made the people despondent. With the country in disarray, the generals staged another coup in June of that year, bringing General Pedro Ramirez (1884 – 1962) to power. His tenure was brief but he succeeded in imposing policies that were even further to the right than ever.

General Edelmiro Farrell (1887 – 1980) replaced him but he was little more than a puppet for Colonel Juan Domingo Perón (1895 – 1974), leader of a Fascist-supporting military faction, Grupo de Oficiales Unidos (GOU). Eventually, Perón became vice president as well as running the ministries of War and Labor.

He won over the Buenos Aires proletariat—the *descamisados* ("shirtless ones") and used their union, the Confederación General de Trabajadores (CGT) as a vehicle for his political ambitions. Suspicious of Perón, the Army arrested him in 1945 and imprisoned him on Martín García Island on the River Plate.

Perón's beautiful and ambitious wife Eva "Evita" Duarte (1919 – 52) rallied support for her husband and the workers took to the streets. Fearful of civil war, the generals released Perón and in February 1946, in an honest election, he was elected President of Argentina. The rule of the "gorillas," as the people called the generals, was over, for the time being.

Ramón S. Castillo served as President of Argentina between 1942 and 1943.

By the age of 14, he was reading Freud as well as the work of the French poet Charles Baudelaire. Alexandre Dumas, Verlaine, and Mallarmé were devoured and later it was the turn of Federico Garcia Lorca and Antonio Machado. Pablo Neruda, the Chilean Communist poet, also became a favorite.

A TEENAGE CRUSH

Asthma had an impact upon the physical appearance of Ernesto, the fits of coughing and breathing difficulties giving him a sunken chest and hunched shoulders. To combat this, he launched a campaign of daily exercise, and engaged in sporting activities such as swimming. He began to play rugby, and became passionate about the game. All of this had the desired results, and he had soon developed a body that would be the envy of any young man.

When it was made clear to Celia and Ernesto Sr. in a number of warning letters from the Argentinean Ministry of Education that they were breaking the law by not sending their son to school, they were forced to enroll him at the Colegio Nacional Dean Funes at Córdoba. This meant a twenty-five-mile bus ride each way. At school, he was teased about his asthma attacks and although he engaged in sports, as ever, he frequently had to run from the field in the middle of an attack to find his inhaler. He was never, therefore, the athlete he aspired to be.

In 1937, Ernesto was confronted by politics on a personal level for the first time when the family of Dr. Juan González Aguilar, who had been in the Spanish Republican Army's medical corps, arrived in Alta Gracia. With their leftist, anti-fascist sympathies, the González Aguilars were natural friends for the Guevaras and Ernesto soon befriended the two González Aguilar children, Carmen and José who was nicknamed Pepe. Ernesto was undoubtedly heavily influenced by the stories they told of life in war-torn Spain.

His interest in the politics of the left and right in Spain was further heightened by other contacts such as the Barral family whose son

Fernando became a firm friend. Fernando and Ernesto together often visited Ernesto's cousin, Carmen Córdova Iturburu, who was the daughter of Celia's older sister and a communist poet, Cayetano Córdova Iturburu.

Cayetano had served in Madrid as a newspaper correspondent on the Loyalist side and Spanish politics were often discussed during the boys' visits. It seems, however, that Ernesto was more intent on enjoying the company of Carmen, or "Negrita" as she was nicknamed, on whom he had a teenage crush.

HATRED AND VIOLENCE AS REVOLUTIONARY TOOLS

Given what he saw in the government of the generals during the early years of his life, it is little wonder that not only did Ernesto Guevara grow up with a disdain for representative democracy but that he also developed a capacity for hatred as well as a predisposition toward violence. He later wrote that he championed:

> *hatred as a weapon of struggle, intransigent hatred for the enemy, which makes the human being exert himself beyond his natural limits and become an effective, violent, selective, and cold killing machine.*

As a teenager, however, he was not active in politics, despite his hatred of the way his country was being run and the people who were in government. When Argentinean schools were purged of democratic teachers in 1943 by the notoriously Fascist Minister of Education, Gustavo Martínez Zuviría, he failed to join protestors. And he does not seem to have taken part in the student strikes during the war years against fascist and anti-Semitic movements.

He also did not protest against the Perón dictatorship despite being, like his parents, a fervent *antiperonista*. At the University of Buenos Aires, he became a member of the militant socialist Federacion Universitaria de Buenos Aires (FUBA) but does not appear to have contributed much to its activities.

CHAPTER 2

DOCTOR ERNESTO GUEVARA

In 1947, at age 19, Ernesto Guevara enrolled at Buenos Aires University, surprising his family and friends by deciding to take up medicine and not engineering. One reason for this decision seems to have been to learn as much as he could about the asthma that was blighting his life. Perhaps, he thought, he could even find a cure for it and make his name as a great scientist.

As soon as he had the requisite qualifications he found a position with the pioneering Argentinean allergist Salvador Pisani. Ernesto had already met Dr. Pisani as a patient and had been impressed by the fact that, as a result of his treatment, there was an improvement in his condition.

Another reason for entering medical research may have been a desire to help his mother who had by this time been diagnosed with cancer. The research job did not last long, however, and one can only surmise that he was not excited by the long, tiresome hours in the laboratory. University, likewise, bored him and he squeezed through his exams without setting the world alight.

José Hernández.

MARTÍN FIERRO

● ● ● ● ● ● ● ● ● ● ●

Also known as *El Gaucho Martín Fierro*, José Hernández's 2,316-line epic poem was published in two parts, the first, *El Gaucho Martín Fierro* in 1872, the second, *La Vuelta de Martín Fierro* in 1879. It celebrates the role played by the gaucho—the Argentine equivalent of the American cowboy—in Argentina's struggle for independence from Spain.

The Spanish in which it is written is the type spoken in rural Argentina and it is widely recognized as the greatest poem of the genre known as "gauchesque" poetry, and is a proud emblem of Argentine national identity.

The poem was hugely popular and by the time the second part was published, 48,000 copies of the first had been sold in Argentina and Uruguay and it was being read aloud as a form of public entertainment. Nowadays, the Martin Fierro Awards are the most prestigious awards for radio and television.

DODGING NATIONAL SERVICE

His spare time was spent reading poetry and playing chess. He especially enjoyed *Martín Fierro*, a long epic poem written by the Argentine writer José Hernández (1834 – 86), memorizing and reciting it to friends. Chess was very popular among young Argentineans at this time and Ernesto played whenever he could, and continued to play later in life also. It was just as well he had chess to occupy him because by this time his asthma made playing rugby impossible.

All Argentine boys were required to register for military service at age 18, and despite his asthma, Ernesto was afraid that he would be conscripted. He was, after all, a robust young man. He decided, therefore, to ensure that he had a severe asthma attack when he was due to appear before the military doctors for his medical examination. Before he went, he took an ice-cold shower and when he was stricken by an attack in the examination room, he was duly excused service.

It seems odd, given his medical condition, but around this time, he started to smoke special cigarettes for asthmatics and he would later move on to smoking Havana cigars which seemed to help relax him.

A FAMILY CRISIS

Ernesto Sr. was not wealthy enough to fund his oldest son through university which necessitated the boy finding work. He was, however, well-connected in Buenos Aires and he used his contacts to find gainful employment for his son. This was something the Guevaras hated as it was what their political enemies did, using influence and position to gain an advantage in a government that the family detested.

But political sentiment did not stop Ernesto Sr. in this case. The job was in the municipal government of the city. It was easy and hardly stretched Ernestito. There were days, he later recalled, when there was nothing to do and he estimated that seventy-five percent of the people employed there were superfluous.

At this point in his life his real passion was travel and he escaped the heat of the city whenever he could, hitch-hiking or cycling into the surrounding countryside. But at home, things were bad. The last of the *mate* plantation holdings had been sold in 1947 and two years later, the family finances, or rather the lack of them, had persuaded them to relocate to a place Celia owned in Buenos Aires. It was then the marriage effectively ended.

They had been quarreling for years, over Ernestito's treatment, or over politics. These disagreements had often threatened to become violent and Celia is said to have carried a gun to be used against her husband. Ernesto Sr.'s extramarital affairs did not help the situation and Celia was not the type of woman to turn a blind eye to his escapades.

Ernesto Guevara, 1947.

CÓRDOBA

● ● ● ● ● ● ● ● ●

Córdoba is about twenty-five miles from Alta Gracia, more or less in the country's geographical center. Buenos Aires lies 435 miles to the southeast. The capital of the province of the same name, it is Argentina's second most populous city.

It was first settled in 1570 by Jéronimo Luis de Cabrera (1528 – 74) under the auspices of the Spanish viceroy, Francisco de Toledo (1515 – 82) who sent a one hundred-man expedition which arrived on the site of the future city on June 24, 1573. Twelve days later Córdoba de la Nueva Andalucía was founded.

The natives of the area, the Comechingones, resisted the settlers, making repeated attacks on their fort for four years before the Spanish relocated to the opposite bank of the Suquía River in 1577. A city with a grid of seventy blocks was laid out and Córdoba began to be transformed into a successful trading center, doing business with the cities in the north of the colony.

The Jesuits arrived in 1599 and the college they established in 1610 became the University of Córdoba three years later, the Americas'

fourth-oldest university. By 1760, the population had risen to 22,000. Toward the end of the nineteenth century, there was an upsurge in European immigration, mostly from the Italian regions of Piedmont, Lombardy, and Veneto, and Spain—Galicians and Basques. Córdoba became increasingly industrial. With British investment and the growth of the railways, leather, meat, and wool became the principal exports. In 1927 the Military Aircraft Manufacturer FMA was established and it became one of the most important facilities in the world with the contribution of German technical experts.

In 1947 the population was 400,000, but the development of new industries in the city led to an influx of people from the countryside, doubling the population. It became increasingly politically influential, and was the scene of the initial mutiny that deposed President Juan Perón in 1955. The "Cordobazo" of 1969, a series of violent protests by workers and students, led to the elections of 1973 that brought the Justicialist Party of Héctor Cámpora (1909 – 80) to power. The city is now home to more than 1.3 million people.

The Ernesto Che Guevara Museum at the Guevara's old house in Alta Gracia, near Córdoba, Argentina.

The struggle to bring up and educate five children on meager finances undoubtedly placed further stress on their relationship. The family moved into Celia's property but Ernesto Sr. rented an apartment elsewhere and the children rarely saw him.

THE OBJECT OF HIS DESIRE

For the first time in his young life Ernesto was in love. The object of his desire was very different to him. The beautiful Maria del Carmen Ferreyra (born 1934), known to her acquaintances as Chichina, was the daughter of one of the richest men in Córdoba, a representative of the wealthy and privileged elite that the Guevara family hated. They were part of the ruling class of Argentina and responsible, in Ernesto's eyes, for the corruption and social problems that blighted his country.

The family lived in a grand house, one of the most imposing buildings in the city, and also owned an estate at Malagueño that boasted polo fields, swimming pools, tennis courts, and stables. There was a village which was home to the workers who mined the lime quarries owned by the family. She was indeed a strange choice for this restless, rebellious young man.

Naturally, Chichina's mother and father were horrified by their daughter's relationship with Ernesto and this made the relationship futile from the start. Chichina may have reciprocated his feelings for her, but there was no way it could run its course, so opposed were her parents to him. This only helped increase his antipathy to the establishment and its values.

BEAUTY AND THE BEAST

Ernesto had been introduced to Chichina by his cousin Negrita and must have been immediately of concern to her parents as soon as they laid eyes on him. He was a casual dresser in the extreme, wearing baggy trousers, sometimes held up by string, often dirty shirts, scruffy shoes, and ragged, tangled hair. He looked like a tramp, especially when he was in

Ernesto Guevara and Chichina Ferreyra around 1950.

the company of the elegantly dressed upper-classes surrounding his attractive girlfriend.

His table manners were appalling. He was nicknamed "El Chancho" (the Pig) by his friends, due to the noise he made when he ate. And he did not hold back on expressing his opinions when among these representatives of the elite, giving full voice to his disgust at what he saw as their leeching off the state. He eagerly launched himself into arguments with them.

He was different to them and that is perhaps what attracted Chichina to him. She enjoyed watching the shocked reaction of her family and friends to his contrary views and his shabby suits. She said later:

> He fascinated me. His obstinate look and his irreverent nature. His sloppy dress made us laugh and, at the same time, feel a little ashamed.

FLAT-FOOTED AND TONE-DEAF

Of course, Chichina was also impressed by his intelligence, his ability to discuss a wide range of topics or recite poetry from memory. She tried to teach him to dance, but although he visited the capital's tango clubs and watched couples glide across the floor on many occasions, he was flat-footed and lacked any understanding of rhythm. He could not sing either. He was tone-deaf and what emerged from his mouth was always excruciatingly flat.

Ernesto's relationship with Chichina lasted almost ten years, from the mid-1940s until he left Argentina for good in 1953, although it was more difficult to maintain after the Guevaras moved to Buenos Aires. The two corresponded but it was hard to retain the ardor of their relationship by post. It has even been suggested that the two became engaged around 1948 or 1949 but there is no real evidence for this, and neither do we know if their respective families were informed about it.

JOURNEY TO THE NORTH

In the summer of 1950, Ernesto decided to embark on his first long journey by a motorized bicycle. Taking two changes of clothes, a thermos bottle, a few tins of food, and toiletries, he bade farewell to Chichina in Córdoba and traveled to the north-western provinces of Jujuy and Salta that bordered Bolivia. On his 4,500-mile journey he encountered much poverty, disease, and starvation among the Indian tribes who inhabited those regions. It stirred his social conscience and his stubbornness. Against all advice, he crossed the vast salt flats of Salinas Grandes with just a half-liter of water.

Ernesto Guevara, 1950.

CHAPTER 3

THE MOTORCYCLE DIARIES

In September 1951, Ernesto visited his old friend Alberto Granado in Córdoba. Together they had fantasized when they were younger about making a grand tour of Latin America, as Alberto later explained:

> *To travel around Latin America, to know its beauties and the misery in which its inhabitants live, was a dream long fondly dreamed by us, and our future journey was the obligatory subject of conversation during those nights I passed with Guevara and my brothers in some mountain region, on some weekend, or some excursion.*

Alberto was now finally ready to undertake this romantic voyage of exploration on his motorcycle La Poderosa, but his brother Tomás was unable to go with him and he wondered who he should take. Naturally, when Ernesto heard his plans, he was eager to accompany him, but there was an obstacle in his way—the medical exams he had to take in December. Passing these exams was essential to his progress in medicine.

But he need not have worried. His friend agreed to wait until he had taken the exams. There was another problem however. He had to talk the trip through with his mother who would naturally be concerned for his safety on such a serious undertaking. She was also concerned about him finishing his course.

Brothers Tomás and Alberto Granado (right) pretending to hitch a ride from Ernesto Guevara on his bicycle.

A PROMISE TO CELIA

Celia Guevara was determined that all her children obtain qualifications and three of Ernesto's siblings were studying at university, despite the family's continuing lack of money. The two girls, Ana María and Celia were following in their father's footsteps by studying architecture while Roberto was studying law. So Celia made Ernesto promise that he would return to university after the trip and finish his course. He promised and she gave the venture her blessing.

In December he duly passed his exams and he and Alberto began to make ready for the trip. The motorbike was taken to a garage where it was given an overhaul with new tires and brakes. They piled it high with cooking utensils, their extra clothing, and toiletries. Ernesto also insisted on packing a revolver with them for added security.

GREETINGS FOR THE GRINGOS

There is some confusion about the date of their departure. One friend says that they left in January 1952. Before they departed, some say Ernesto traveled to Miramar on the coast near Buenos Aires to say goodbye to Chichina, even though their romance had definitely cooled.

He gave her a puppy by way of a farewell gift and named it Come-Back, in English. He told her that they might make it as far as the United States and asked her: "Do you want me to extend your greetings to the gringos?" She told him she would rather he bought her a lace dress.

But Alberto maintains that they set out on December 29, 1951, leaving from Córdoba and making for the Andes via Buenos Aires where they bade farewell to Ernesto's family. He makes no mention of a visit to see Chichina or the gift of a dog, so the story may simply be part of the myth of Che Guevara.

Ernesto Guevara (left) holding the handlebars of the 500cc Norton motorcycle which he used on his 1952 journey through South America.

ALBERTO GRANADO

Alberto Granado (1922 – 2011) was born in the province of Córdoba, the son of a Spanish immigrant and trade unionist who had a job on the Argentinean railway. Six years older than Ernesto Guevara, Granado met him through his younger brother Tomás who was a classmate. Ernesto's passion for rugby led him to join a rugby team that Granado put together and the two soon realized that they had a lot in common, sharing a love of literature and a similar view of the world and politics.

Coming from a left-wing, working-class family, Granado was a Marxist at an early age and in 1943 was briefly imprisoned for his opposition to Perón. He studied biochemistry at Córdoba University and while Ernesto was studying medicine in Buenos Aires, he worked at a provincial leprosarium.

Leaving his work at the leprosarium, Granado and Ernesto indulged their shared passion for adventure and travel by journeying around Argentina and Chile on a 1939 Norton 500cc motorbike named La Poderosa II (The Mighty One). When the motorcycle gave up the ghost in Santiago, they went on to travel north by ship, bus, and riverboat. In 1952, they arrived in Venezuela, and Ernesto traveled on to Miami, while Granado remained behind having found a job at the Cabo Blanco leprosarium in Maiquetía.

In 1955 Granado traveled to Europe on a scholarship from the Instituto Superiore di Sanitá in Rome and he also traveled through France and Spain. When he eventually returned to Caracas, he married a Venezuelan woman and began working in the school of biochemistry at the city's university.

After the Cuban Revolution, he was invited to Havana by "Che" Guevara and moved there with his family to take a job at the University of Havana. In 1962, he was co-founder of a new medical school in Santiago de Cuba. That same year, he traveled to Argentina seeking to recruit men to come to Cuba for military training, but the resulting guerrilla campaign in northern Argentina was unsuccessful, and many of the guerrillas were killed.

Giving up revolutionary activity, he returned to medical research. Following the death of his friend Che in 1967, he was appointed director of the genetics department of the National Health Center for Stockbreeding and Farming. He retired in 1994 and died in 2011, at the age of 88.

Aboard their "Mambo-Tango" raft, Ernesto Guevara (right) with Alberto Granado (left) set off down the Amazon River, June 1952.

CROSSING THE ANDES

Their first destination was south Argentina where they hoped the warm dry pampas would work wonders on Ernesto's health. They stopped at ranches and caught glimpses of the life of the gaucho before crossing the Andes. Ernesto photographed everything as they went, La Poderosa's tires were shredded by rough terrain and the engine frequently overheated. Eventually they rolled down to the Chilean capital Santiago.

Alberto always kept a diary when he made such a trip and he persuaded his traveling companion to do the same. Approaching Santiago, La Poderosa's engine finally succumbed and they had to leave the bike behind and carry on as best they could. Alberto later suggested it was the best thing that could happen, saying:

> *Undoubtedly that trip would not have been as useful and beneficial as it was, as a personal experience, if the motor had held out ... This gave us a chance to become familiar with the people. We worked, took on jobs to make money and continue traveling ... We hauled merchandise, carried sacks, worked as sailors, cops and doctors.*

They did not have much money, and did almost anything to keep body and soul together, washing dishes and working as stevedores, baggage handlers, and salesmen, and they also did odd jobs. When they had completely run out of money, they even spent the fifteen dollars Chichina had given Ernesto for the lace dress. As he said at the time: "When it's a question of starving or keeping a promise, I believe that the former has priority."

They hitchhiked into Santiago from where they planned to travel to Easter Island to visit the leprosarium at Rapa Nui. Presenting themselves in Chile as "leprologists," they were interviewed by a local newspaper. They must have laughed when they read the headline "Argentine Experts in Leprology Touring South America on Motorcycle." But they never made it to Easter Island—it was too long to wait for the next boat.

THE JUNGLES OF PERU

They headed north again, across the driest place in the world, the Atacama Desert, and into Peru. Reaching the capital Cusco, they explored the city for a few days before traveling to Machu Picchu, the famous fifteenth-

Machu Picchu, the world-famous Inca site that Ernesto and Alberto visited during their South American motorcycle tour in 1952.

century Inca citadel, fifty miles away. Leaving Machu Picchu, they traveled eleven hours on mules to reach the leprosarium at Huambo, deep in the jungle.

They met Dr. Hugo Pesche and spent time at his leprosarium, then he gave them directions to another leprosy center at San Pablo in the province of Loreto. To get there they had to travel by steamer on the Amazon, setting out from the little port of Pucallpa. But at the river town of Iquitos, Ernesto had a violent asthma attack, brought on, most likely, by the terrible humidity of the region. He was admitted to hospital where he remained for a few days.

When he was well again, they left for San Pablo where the letter of introduction from Dr. Pesche ensured they were warmly received. They were even allowed to work in the center's laboratory. By this time, Ernesto's initial fear of contracting leprosy had diminished and he was able to move freely among the patients.

In fact, he and Alberto played football with the patients and took them on trips out of the center, visiting local villages. They also organized monkey-hunts. By the time they were due to leave the colony they were much loved and the lepers constructed a raft named Mambo-Tango after the dances of their two nations. They sailed downriver to their next destination, the town of Leticia, situated in Colombia on the borders of both Brazil and Peru.

ARRESTED IN BOGOTÁ

They set out on their raft on June 21, 1952, the great rain forest creeping down to the riverbanks on either side of them. Unfortunately, they drifted on past Leticia and had to make their way back there on the boat of a local native. But by this time they had no money and nothing such as a letter of introduction to vouch for them.

They were picked up as suspicious characters by the local authorities but when it was discovered they were Argentinean everything changed. All Argentineans were famed for their soccer skills and it was presumed these two would be no exception. They were hired

as soccer coaches and took the local team to victory in the regional championship. They were paid cash which funded their onward journey to the Colombian capital Bogotá.

Bogotá was a dangerous place. A civil war—known as "La Violencia"—was in full swing, a response to brutal government repression after rioting four years previously. In such a situation, two scruffy strangers were decidedly suspicious and Ernesto and Alberto were arrested almost as soon as they arrived in the city. They rather stupidly got into an argument with police officers and were hauled off to the local police station.

ONE FINAL ADVENTURE

Fortunately, some friendly students interceded on their behalf and obtained their release. The students' advice was that they should get out of Colombia as quickly as they could. They organized a collection for them, raising enough cash to get the two Argentineans to Caracas, capital of Venezuela, where they arrived on July 14.

Alberto managed to find work in a leprosarium and liked it so much that he decided to stay there, leaving Ernesto to return home to fulfil his promise to his mother and complete his studies. But he was offered one final adventure.

He met a relative in Caracas who regularly flew racehorses from Argentina to Venezuela and the United States. He offered to fly Ernesto home when he made his next trip but first he had to make a delivery in Miami. As ever, Ernesto was broke and Miami was an expensive city. Most of the time he spent in a library and lived on coffee.

But in Miami, he managed to buy the dress Chichina had asked for, earning the money from odd jobs. He returned home, age 24, undoubtedly wiser and more mature than when he had left, but he was still no closer to knowing what to do with the rest of his life.

A scene from the movie *The Motorcycle Diaries* (2004) chronicling the trip through South America that Ernesto Guevara and Alberto Granado made in 1952. The movie starred Gael García Bernal (right) as Ernesto Guevara and Rodrigo de la Serna (left) as Alberto Granado.

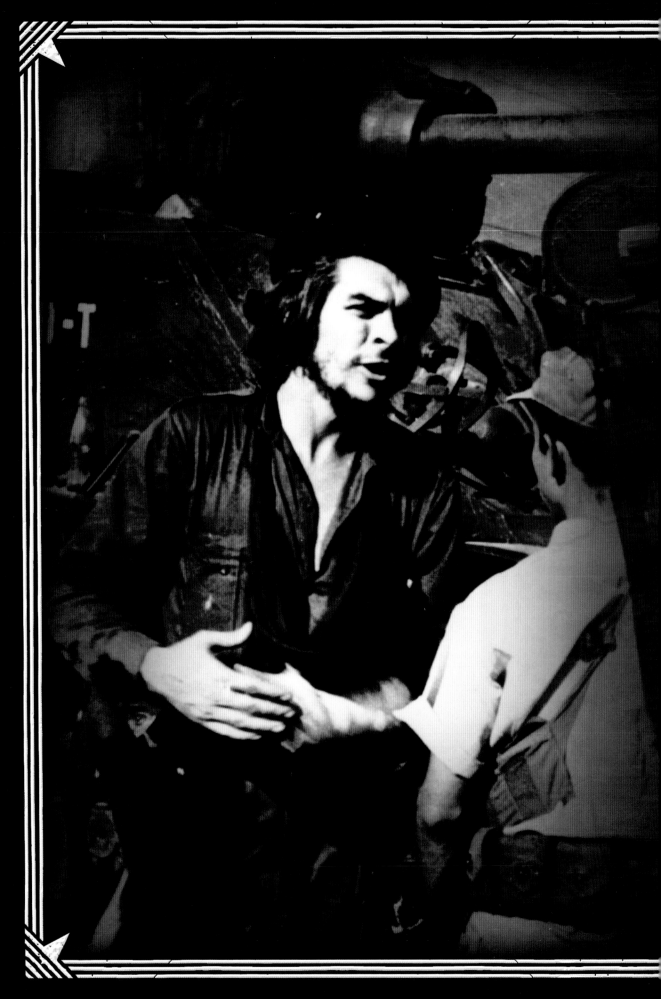

PART TWO
THE ROAD TO REVOLUTION

THE REVOLUTION IS NOT AN
APPLE THAT FALLS WHEN IT IS RIPE.
YOU HAVE TO MAKE IT FALL.

CHE GUEVARA

CHAPTER 4

A SOLDIER OF AMERICA

On his return to Argentina, Ernesto studied for the dozen or so medical exams he had to pass. He started seeing Chichina again and intended to marry her, despite what her parents thought. But when he informed her that he had every intention of meeting up with Alberto again in Caracas, she was unhappy and they argued.

GONE FOR GOOD

Perhaps he was really rebelling against the notion of settling down, or else he was indulging in the fantasy of becoming a famous leprologist. Some said he was afraid Chichina would reject him in the end, following the advice of her parents, and he did not want to wait around for that to happen. Ultimately, it seems unlikely there was any agreement between them about marriage. If Chichina had committed herself to him, there is every chance that Ernesto may have stayed.

Chichina would certainly have had a very different kind of existence had she stuck with this restless individual who wanted to work with lepers. It was a wonderful and generous intention but not one that would have paid for the lifestyle to which Chichina was accustomed. They finally split up in January 1953.

Two months later Ernesto passed his final exams and qualified as a physician-surgeon. Freed of all his obligations, he began to prepare for a third South American odyssey. This time he would be gone for good.

The Moncada Barracks, Santiago de Cuba, the scene of Fidel Castro's infamous attack on July 26, 1953.

TRAVELING TO BOLIVIA

Once again, he had a traveling companion, Carlos "Calica" Ferrer, a childhood friend from Alta Gracia. Given Ernesto's medical condition and the danger of him suffering an attack on the road, it was essential that someone traveled with him. They set off in July 1953.

Toward the end of that same month, a young revolutionary named Fidel Castro launched an unsuccessful armed attack on the Moncada Barracks in Santiago in Cuba.

But such things were far from Ernesto's mind as he traveled by train toward Bolivia and its capital La Paz, 2,000 miles to the north of Buenos Aires. As he took leave of his family at General Belgrano Station in the capital, his last words to them were the fateful: "Here goes a soldier of America."

THE ARROGANCE OF YOUTH

The two arrived in La Paz with not a penny but were fortunate to meet a fellow countryman who fed them. Ernesto appalled his traveling companion with the quantity of food he consumed. He had learned from his previous trip that it was best to eat as much as possible when one could because there would be times when they would be starving.

Revolution had erupted in Bolivia in April 1952 and the new government had launched a series of land reforms that helped to lift the indigenous people out of virtual slavery, giving them freedoms of which they had only ever previously dreamed. Ernesto, however, did not believe that the revolution would succeed as he told the Bolivian Minister of Agriculture when he met him.

He also described the leaders of the National Revolutionary Movement as "opportunists" who were merely hungry for power. It is unknown where these views came from as he had only just arrived in the country and knew little of Bolivian history. Perhaps it can be put down to the arrogance of youth.

LOOKING FOR ADVENTURE

Away from politics, he photographed ancient pre-Incan ruins on the 13,000-feet-high Altiplano, especially Tiahuanaco on the shores of Lake Titicaca. They were now traveling with another Argentinean, Ricardo Rojo (1923 – 95), who had been forced into exile due to his anti-Perónist activities in Argentina. Rojo gave Ernesto a crash course in Latin American politics and tried to persuade him to travel with him to Guatemala where another revolution had begun, instead of visiting Alberto Granado in Caracas.

Ernesto Guevara (left) and Ricardo Rojo on the road in Peru, 1953.

The three crossed into Peru but were waylaid by customs officers at the border because of the revolutionary books and pamphlets in their bags. Eventually, when they had convinced the authorities they were not agitators, they were allowed into the country. Ernesto and Carlos made for Cusco while Rojo set out for Lima where he would wait for them. The three reunited in the capital and boarded a bus that took them northward along the Peruvian coast to Ecuador where they arrived on September 26, 1953.

Their destination was Guayanquil where they met another three Argentineans who were also on the road looking for adventure. They were Oscar Valdovinos, Eduardo "Gualo" García, and Andro Herrero. The six of them had sufficient funds between them to rent a room near the city's busy harbor.

Once again, they had to pass through Colombia for which visas were required. The country was in turmoil, the President of Colombia, Laureano Gómez, had been ousted by Army General Gustavo Rojas Pinilla in a successful *coup d'état*. The General had amassed widespread popular support by promising he would end "La Violencia," which was still raging in the country.

The Colombian authorities were reluctant to issue visas to the Argentineans and the only way they could get them was by producing plane tickets for Bogotá. This meant they could prove they would not be passing through the most dangerous part of the country.

Rojo got help from a lawyer to obtain tickets for ships of the United Fruit Company's Great White Fleet. They traveled in pairs and by this time, Ernesto had been persuaded to see the Guatemalan Revolution in action.

TALK OF REVOLUTION

Traveling on the Great White Fleet with "Gualo" García, Ernesto reached Panama but faced a long journey through Central America to get to Guatemala. He sold his books and wrote some articles for a Panamanian magazine about Machu Picchu to scrape together the necessary funds. These were the first examples of his professional writing.

Ernesto and García made it to San José, the Costa Rican capital, where they met members of an organization called the Caribbean Legion, a loosely associated group of Latin American revolutionaries.

Among this group in Costa Rica at the time were three men who went on to become presidents of their respective countries— Rómulo Betancourt and Raúl Leoni of Venezuela, and Juan Bosch of the Dominican Republic. Ernesto got on particularly well with Juan Bosch, but he did not see eye to eye with Betancourt.

With Bosch, a cultured man, he was able to talk South American literature; with Betancourt, it was usually politics and they did not agree. Betancourt acknowledged the United States' imperialist aspirations, for instance, but was also sympathetic toward the great northern neighbor. Ernesto, on the other hand, was hard-line and hated America, seeing only its expansionist aims.

His first contact with the Cuban Revolution was by chance. He went into a bar in San José and sat at a table next to a loud group of Cubans, survivors of an attack by Fidel Castro's forces on the Moncada Barracks in Santiago, Cuba. This armed attack in 1953 is widely accepted as the beginning of the Cuban Revolution. The date on which the attack took place, July 26, was adopted by Castro as the name of his revolutionary movement— *Movimiento 26 Julio*.

As they talked of the revolution and the dreadful repression in Cuba under the government of Fulgencio Batista, Ernesto heard the name Fidel Castro for the first time. But he doubted the truth of what he was listening to and accused the Cubans of exaggerating, shouting over to them: "Well and good, *muchachos*. And why not tell us a cowboy story?"

THE CARIBBEAN LEGION

• • • • • • • • • • •

The Caribbean Legion was formed with the aim of bringing down dictatorships in Central America and replacing them with democratic governments. It began work in 1946 after the end of World War II.

Democracy had been introduced in several Latin American countries, including Guatemala and Venezuela, and this encouraged the people of other countries to pursue democratic government. At the same time, there were some particularly tyrannical regimes operating in the continent, most notably those of Anastasio Somoza García in Nicaragua and Rafael Trujillo in the Dominican Republic. These became prime targets of the Caribbean Legion's work.

Similar to today's various terrorist networks, the Legion was a very loosely associated multinational organization without any kind of formal structure. It did not even have a name until American journalists coined the term "Caribbean Legion" in 1947. The Dominican Republic, suffering under Trujillo's regime, provided the greatest number of members, but every nation in Latin America was represented.

Members were often veterans of World War II, many Cubans and Dominicans having fought in the United States Army. Others had fought in the Spanish Civil War. Their weapons came from arms dealers who had stocks left after the end of the war and were happy to sell them to the Legion. The Cuban and Guatemalan governments also provided support as well as the government of Costa Rica under José Figueres Ferrer who came to power in 1948. The greatest source of funding, however, was a private individual, Juan Rodriguez Garcia, a wealthy exiled Dominican rancher.

Fidel Castro was a notable member of the Caribbean Legion. He was captured in 1947 during an aborted invasion of the Dominican Republic by 1,200 men of the Legion, in an incident that became known as the Cayo Confites Affair. He managed to escape by leaping from the Cuban Navy vessel on which he was being held.

The Legion collapsed after a disastrous airborne invasion of the Dominican Republic failed in 1949, and never took up arms again.

A 21-year-old Fidel Castro delivering a speech in 1947.

FIDEL CASTRO

Born in 1926, Fidel Alejandro Castro Ruz was the son of Lina Ruz from Pinar del Río in Cuba, and Angel Castro, an immigrant from Spanish Galicia who was a wealthy landowner. Castro received a Jesuit education and went on to study law at Havana University. A brilliant orator, he seemed destined to be a politician, but the *coup d'état* that returned the dictator Fulgencio Batista to power in Cuba in 1952 blocked his way.

Instead he became involved in revolutionary activities and on July 26, 1953, led a band of men in a raid on the Moncada Barracks, Santiago, Cuba's largest military base. The attack was a disaster and many of the revolutionaries perished or were taken prisoner. Castro was sentenced to fifteen years in prison and his brother Raúl, also involved in the attack, received a thirteen-year sentence.

LAUNCHING THE REVOLUTION

Two years later there was an amnesty and Castro was banished into exile in Mexico where he began to assemble a force of armed revolutionaries to fight Batista. One of those who joined him was Ernesto "Che" Guevara. In December 1956 this force landed on Cuba. By January 1959 they had defeated Batista's army and taken control of the country.

At age just 30, Castro arrived in Havana in triumph to launch the Cuban Revolution. Influenced by Marxism, Castro was anti-American, although not communist. However America's displeasure with the turn of events resulted in a failed invasion attempt at the Bay of Pigs. Bungled by the CIA, the incompetent operation wrecked the early months of the presidency of John F. Kennedy.

Hostility between the United States and Cuba reached its zenith with the Cuban Missile Crisis of October 1962. Soviet premier, Nikita Khrushchev tried to install missiles with nuclear warheads on Cuban soil. After a tense few days with the world on the brink of nuclear warfare, Khrushchev ordered the withdrawal of the missiles.

During this incident, Castro was little more than a bit player as the decisions were all taken in Washington and Moscow. His regime survived, of course, but from then on he was fiercely independent in his dealings. He was forced to rely on Russia, however, while also trying to form alliances elsewhere.

BLOCKADES AND SHORTAGES

Meanwhile, attacks on Cuba by the CIA continued and they made many attempts to assassinate Castro. An economic blockade imposed by the United States meant that Cuba was deprived of any contact with the American mainland and there were severe shortages of vegetables, machinery, and technology.

A blockade on shipments of oil was particularly damaging to the Cuban economy. The Soviet Union stepped in to help, but times were undoubtedly hard for the Cuban people. Instead of the country diversifying its agricultural production away from only sugar, Cubans had to focus on sugar production as a mainstay to make the repayments to Moscow.

CRISIS AND EMERGENCY

Under Castro, Cuba was an early member of the Non-Aligned Movement which was an organization that attempted to mobilize emerging nations in a common political purpose. Castro welcomed many African revolutionary leaders to Havana. Cuba also sent troops to Angola and Ethiopia.

Perestroika and *glasnost* in the Soviet Union meant huge problems for Cuba, especially as the United States had told the Russians that Soviet financial help to Cuba would damage future economic aid the Russians would receive from the USA. Typically, Castro declared a state of emergency, improvising brilliantly and describing Cuba as the world's first "green" society. Industry was powered by wind and bicycles became the main means of transport. Then, when communism collapsed, Castro faced a huge crisis as he was no longer able to rely on the Russians, especially as the first President of the Russian Federation Boris Yeltsin was no friend of Cuba during his premiership from 1991 to 1999.

MARRIED TO THE REVOLUTION

Cuba got through the crisis by welcoming tourists and running a dual economy with the US dollar being most important. The emergence of Hugo Chavez as leader in oil-rich Venezuela brought relief and aid to the island when Chavez sent hundreds of thousands of barrels of oil to Cuban refineries.

Although there were women in Castro's life, he always claimed to be married to the revolution. He had married in 1948 and had a son, but divorce followed a few years later. He married again in 1980 and had five sons as well as other children outside marriage. After forty-six years at the helm, Castro handed over power to his brother Raúl in 2006 as his health deteriorated. He died in November 2016, at age 90.

JUAN BOSCH

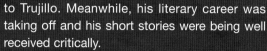

Politician, short story writer, essayist, and educator, Juan Emilio Bosch Gaviño was born in the Dominican Republic in 1909. The son of a Catalan father and a Puerto Rican mother, his family had immigrated from Galicia in Spain.

When President Rafael Trujillo was in power, Bosch was imprisoned for his political opposition to him and when released in 1938, he left the country going into exile in Puerto Rico. From there he moved to Cuba and with other Dominican exiles, he founded the Partido Revolucionario Dominicano (PRD) in opposition to Trujillo. Meanwhile, his literary career was taking off and his short stories were being well received critically.

Bosch was one of the organizers of the Caribbean League's expedition of 1947 that tried unsuccessfully to unseat Trujillo and he fled to Venezuela after its failure. Returning to Cuba, he became involved in the politics of Havana, promoting social reform and writing speeches for President Carlos Prío Socarrás. Bosch was jailed after Batista ousted Socarrás in a coup in 1952. When he was freed, he traveled to Costa Rica and became an educator and led the PRD.

After Trujillo was assassinated in 1961, Bosch returned to the Dominican Republic to be elected President, the people were impressed by his honesty and his direct approach. He immediately launched reforms with a new, more liberal constitution that benefited workers, trade unions, pregnant women, the homeless, farmers, and the young.

His attempts to break up large, private estates angered landowners, and industrialists were unhappy at the new rights for workers. The military were opposed to him and the United States was wary of a left-leaning president.

His presidency lasted just seven months. In September 1963, he was replaced by a military junta and went back into exile in Puerto Rico. Two years later, when there were moves to have him reinstated, the United States sent 42,000 troops to the Dominican Republic to bolster the anti-Bosch forces.

He returned in 1966 to fight an election but was defeated by Joaquín Balaguer. In 1973 he left the PRD and founded the Dominican Liberal Party but lost five presidential elections between 1978 and 1994. Finally at age 83, he retired from politics. Juan Bosch died in 2001, at the age of 92.

RÓMULO BETANCOURT

Rómulo Ernesto Betancourt (1908 – 81) was born in Guatire, near the capital city Caracas in Venezuela. As a young man he was expelled from the country for radical agitation and moved to Costa Rica. In the 1930s, he became one of the main militants of the Communist Party in Costa Rica, before returning to Venezuela to found Acción Democrática (AD) in 1941, the first modern political party in Venezuelan history.

After a military *coup d'état*, Betancourt became president in 1945. He declared that all adult citizens regardless of income, race or ethnicity had the right to vote in elections, and by changes in the taxation system, he ring-fenced half of all foreign oil companies' profits for the Venezuelan exchequer.

In 1948, Betancourt was ousted by another coup and went into exile in New York. He traveled extensively, living in Cuba, Costa Rica, and Puerto Rico, but remained a leader of the opposition-in-exile to the Venezuelan dictatorship of Marcos Pérez Jiménez.

After a 1958 coup Betancourt was elected president for a second time. But Communist revolutionaries began a campaign against him including sabotage, bombings, and kidnappings. It turned out that Cuba was behind the violence, supplying weapons and inciting revolution. Betancourt protested to the OAS, getting Cuba thrown out and making a life-long enemy of Fidel Castro.

Dominican Republic's dictator Rafael Trujillo also hated Betancourt and supported many plots by Venezuelan exiles to overthrow him including a car bomb attempt on his life in 1960. Betancourt was badly injured and public opinion turned against Trujillo, who was assassinated by his own people in the Dominican Republic a year later in 1961.

Betancourt's greatest achievement was the 1963 elections during which he became Venezuela's first democratically-elected president with a 90 percent turn-out of the electorate. It was unprecedented for a nation that had been controlled by dictators for most of its history.

In 1964 Betancourt was awarded a lifetime seat in Venezuela's senate, due to his status as a former president. His later life was given over to writing and spending time with his wife Dr. Reneé Hartmann. He died on September 18, 1981, at age 73.

CHAPTER 5

A CHANCE TO CHANGE THE WORLD

Ernesto Guevara finally reached Guatemala in December 1953. Like Bolivia, it was a country in turmoil. Under the leadership of Colonel Jacobo Arbenz Guzmán, Guatemala was heading toward total communism. Ernesto found this unstoppable rush to communism exhilarating. He wanted to become involved, especially as by this time he was undoubtedly a Marxist, a view supported by one of Fidel Castro's followers, Mario Dalmau who was exiled in Guatemala at the same time: "He had read widely in Marx and Lenin, a whole Marxist library, and his thought was clearly Marxist." His future wife, Hilda Gadea Acosta agreed: "With regard to theory, Che was already defined."

He quickly made contact with people in the Arbenz government through acquaintances in Buenos Aires and was introduced to the right people. The Foreign Minister Raúl Osegueda paid his rent and introduced him to the Health Ministry where, with his medical qualification, he hoped to find work. They disappointed him by insisting that he had to be a member of the Communist Party to be employed. He refused to join the party, insisting that he was a revolutionary and did not believe in affiliation to any political party. He never did work in Guatemala.

A POWERFUL INFLUENCE

Hilda Gadea was perhaps the most important woman to enter Ernesto's life. Most significantly she introduced him to the Cuban rebels of Fidel Castro. She lived in the same boarding house in Guatemala City as Ernesto and Rojo and worked at the time, like many of the exiles, for the Instituto de Fomento de Produccíon (INFOP), a government body that was set up to develop industrial expansion.

She was earning a decent living and Ernesto was making a meager income from the sale of magazines and books. She helped him financially and even paid his rent when the Foreign Minister's generosity ended.

Short and stocky with olive skin and straight black hair, she was the complete opposite of Chichina in appearance. But she was a committed revolutionary with a lot of political experience and she was soon a powerful central influence on Ernesto's life. Before long they became lovers.

Ernesto was still fascinated by archaeology and visited many ancient sites, often with Rojo and Hilda, but he was increasingly consumed by politics. Hilda introduced him to Nico López, a close associate of Fidel Castro, who had led another attack at the same time as Castro's men were attacking the Moncada Barracks. López explained the objectives of Castro's movement and Ernesto began to give the Cubans a little more respect than before, and was persuaded to support Castro's cause.

UP FOR THE FIGHT

As the Guatemalan Revolution came to an end with troops approaching Guatemala City, Hilda remembered Ernesto was eager to fight. She recalled him asking "to go to the front to fight but nobody paid attention to him." He did, however, join groups defending the capital when there were what Hilda called "bombardments" (bombardments of leaflets, that is) being dropped on the city's inhabitants.

Hilda Gadea Acosta (1925 – 74) was a revolutionary leader and economist who was multi-lingual, very politicized, and highly intellectual. Born in Lima, Peru, she had Chinese and indigenous Indian ancestry. She worked in Peru as the first female secretary and leader of a Marxist political party but because of her activism she was forced to leave the country in 1948. She went into exile in Guatemala where she became a communist.

She met Ernesto Guevara in Guatemala in 1953, when she was 28 and he was 25. They moved to Mexico where she was responsible for introducing him to Castro's Cuban revolutionaries. She became pregnant with his child in summer 1955 and the two were married that year. The couple's daughter, Hilda "Hildita" Beatriz Guevara Gadea was born in February 1956.

Ernesto left Hilda and his daughter behind when he went off to fight in Cuba but after the success of the revolution, he invited them both to Havana. When Hilda arrived she was faced with the fact that there was another woman in her husband's life—Aleida March, a female revolutionary fighter.

They were divorced in June 1959 but Hilda stayed on in Havana where she worked and wrote, and remained loyal to her ex-husband's political movement. She died in 1974 at age 48.

THE GUATEMALAN REVOLUTION

● ● ● ● ● ● ● ● ● ●

The Guatemalan Revolution is the ten-year period in Guatemalan history between the 1944 overthrow of the dictator Jorge Ubico and the 1954 *coup d'état* organized by the United States that removed President Jacobo Arbenz from power. It was the only time between 1930 and the end of the Guatemalan Civil War in 1996 when democracy prevailed in the Central American country. Government from the late nineteenth century until 1944 had been authoritarian.

The American corporation the United Fruit Company became a very powerful agency within the country when they began trading in tropical fruit. They received significant government concessions and dispossessed many indigenous people, transforming their land into banana plantations. The process of dispossession was at its height during Jorge Ubico's presidency from 1931 to 1944. His term of office also saw brutal repression, dreadful labor conditions, and the imposition of a police state.

Ubico was forced to resign in June 1944 by a pro-democracy movement made up of students and workers but he installed a three-man military junta in his place that persevered with his cruel policies. In October 1944 Jacobo Arbenz toppled the junta in a coup that became known as the "October Revolution." The ensuing elections were overwhelmingly won by Juan José Arévalo who began a program of social reform.

Foreign estates were confiscated and the land redistributed to the peasants. Landowners were forced by law to provide adequate housing for workers, and new homes, hospitals, and schools were built. By 1951 Arévalo had survived twenty-five coup attempts, and in the election that year, Jacobo Arbenz became president winning a landslide victory. He continued the work of his predecessor and launched an ambitious land-reform program.

The United Fruit Company lost some of its land as a result of the reforms and persuaded the US government to get rid of the president. The CIA orchestrated a *coup d'état* claiming Arbenz was a communist and a threat to the security of the region. He was removed from power and replaced by a military junta. A brutal civil war ensued which lasted thirty-six years from 1960 to 1996.

Insurgent soldiers reacting to gunfire during the Guatemalan Revolution.

Dalmau recalls that Ernesto joined the defense guards of the Alianza de la Juventud Democrática—the youth wing of one of the leftist political parties fighting to keep Arbenz in power. In 1958, Ernesto described his role at the time to an Argentinean newspaper:

> I never held any post in [Arbenz's] government. But when the North American invasion developed, I tried to form a group of young men like myself to confront the frutero adventurers of United Fruit. In Guatemala it was necessary to fight and almost nobody fought.

Eventually, as the enemy came closer, he had to seek shelter in the Argentine embassy in the city. By this time he was convinced that there needed to be an armed struggle against the forces of imperialism. However he still saw himself not as a soldier with a gun in his hand but as a doctor serving the revolution with his skills:

> I had traveled much—it was during these moments in Guatemala, the Guatemala of Arbenz—and I had begun to make a few notes on the regulation of the conduct of the revolutionary physician. I began to inquire what was necessary to become a revolutionary physician. However, the aggression came, the aggression which would loose United Fruit, the Department of State, Foster Dulles—in reality it is the same. I then realized a fundamental thing: to be a revolutionary doctor there must first be a revolution.

BECOMING CHE GUEVARA

Around this time, Ernesto Guevara became Che Guevara, gradually taking on the name and the revolutionary persona by which he came to be known. In Argentina, "che" is a common greeting for a friend or acquaintance. It seems as if Ernesto's Cuban friends found Ernesto a little formal and they all had *noms de guerre* when they went into battle. For Ernesto's part, he enjoyed the sobriquet:

> For me, "Che" signifies what is most important, most loved in my life. How could I not like it? Everything that went before, my name, my surname, are small things, personal, insignificant things.

THE UNITED FRUIT COMPANY AND THE BANANA REPUBLICS

• • • • • • • • • • •

The United Fruit Company traded in tropical fruit (mainly bananas) from Central and South America, selling their produce into the United States and Europe. The company was formed in 1899 and flourished in the early and mid-twentieth century. Sanctioned by corrupt governments they dispossessed local peasant farmers of their property, acquiring control over immense territories of land, and dominating the banana trade in Central America and the Caribbean. The virtual monopoly they held gave rise to certain regions such as Costa Rica, Honduras, and Guatemala being called banana republics.

A worker carries a stem of bananas over his shoulder on a United Fruit Company plantation, Tiquisate, Guatemala, 1945.

THE REVOLUTIONARY LIFE

Traveling to Mexico, Che was not only getting closer geographically to his revolutionary fate, he was also getting closer philosophically. He arrived on September 21, 1954, telling officials as he entered the country that he was a tourist.

In the Argentinean embassy in Guatemala City, he had been offered a safe passage back to Argentina by the Perón government which he had rejected. He would not be able to exact revenge for the overthrow of Arbenz in Buenos Aires. Personally, Chichina was gone forever, but he now had Hilda urging him on toward revolution.

Mexico was the ideal place because although its own revolution had taken place more than three decades previously, it was still a hub for revolutionaries. Che hoped to renew his friendship with the Cuban rebels who seemed to him to be the way into a revolution that might prove more successful than Guatemala. Through their activities he might be able to strike a blow against the hated United States. He summed up his loathing for the imperialism of America in an article he wrote after Arbenz had been removed from office—"I Witnessed the Fall of Jacobo Arbenz."

BAD PHOTOS IN MEXICO CITY

In Mexico City Che's first concern was earning some money so that he could live. He really only had one contact there, a Guatemalan communist Julio Roberto Cáceres Vallé, who was nicknamed "El Patojo" (Guatemalan slang for "child") because of his diminutive stature. Che was very fond of this man who would die fighting in Guatemala in later years. He and El Patojo pulled their resources together to help each other, as Che described later:

El Patojo had no money and I had only a few pesos. I bought a camera and, together, we dedicated ourselves to the illegal work of taking photographs in the parks, in association with a Mexican who had a small darkroom where we developed them. We knew the whole city

of Mexico, walking about it from one end to the other to deliver the bad photographs we took, fighting with all sorts of customers to convince them that really the little child in the photograph looked handsome and it was worthwhile paying a peso for this marvel. This employment enabled us to eat for several months, and gradually we fared better, until the demands of the revolutionary life separated us.

ENCOUNTERING FIDEL CASTRO

Hilda duly arrived in Mexico City and moved in with Che. She fell pregnant and their daughter Hildita was born in February 1956. Now for the first time, Che found work as a doctor. Through influential contacts, he started a job in the allergy department of Mexico City's General Hospital. He also took up a position teaching at the National Autonomous University of Mexico, later moving on to a better job at the Institute of Cardiology.

It was while working at the General Hospital that he once more made the acquaintance of his lost Cuban friends when Nico López walked in with a man who needed treatment. A few days later, Nico introduced Che to Raúl Castro, one of the survivors of the Moncada raid who had recently been released from prison by President Batista.

Che was invited to meet Fidel Castro in an historic meeting that took place in a small apartment in Mexico City that Raúl shared with his brother, owned by Cuban exile María Antonia González. Her house became the general headquarters of the Cuban Revolution as Fidel Castro and his followers formed the 26th of July Movement, and prepared to take back their homeland from Batista. Che later wrote of his first meeting with the man with whom his future would be irrevocably linked:

I met him on one of those cold nights in Mexico, and I remember our first conversation on international politics. Within a few hours—at dawn—I was one of his future expeditionaries.

RAÚL CASTRO

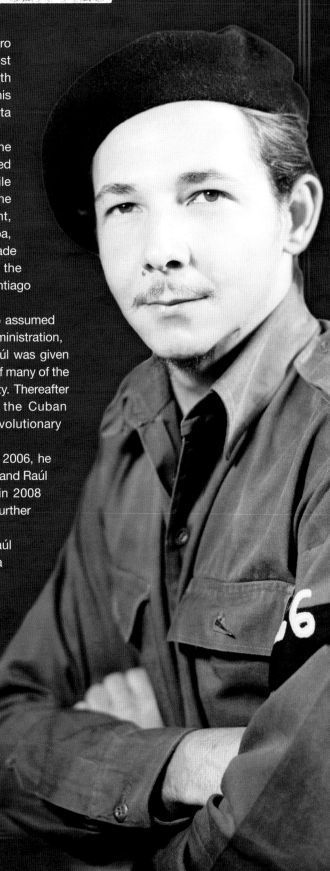

Fidel Castro's younger brother Raúl Modesto Castro Ruz (born 1931) has been a committed socialist since he was a young man. He joined the youth wing of the Cuban Communist Party and, with his brother, took part in protests against the Batista government that often turned violent.

After participating in the infamous raid on the Moncada Barracks in 1953, Raúl was imprisoned for twenty-two months and then went into exile in Mexico where the Castro brothers formed the revolutionary group, the 26th of July Movement, with Che Guevara. After the rebels landed in Cuba, Raúl was one of the twelve combatants who made it to safety in the Sierra Maestra. Later he led the Cuban rebels to victory when they captured Santiago de Cuba.

After Batista's overthrow in 1959 Fidel Castro assumed military and political power in Cuba. Under his administration, Cuba became a one-party communist state. Raúl was given the task of supervising the trials and executions of many of the captives, estimated at between thirty and seventy. Thereafter Raúl held multiple leading positions within the Cuban government and served as Minister of the Revolutionary Armed Forces from 1959 until 2008.

When Fidel Castro underwent surgery in July 2006, he handed his executive powers over to his brother, and Raúl took over the presidency on a full-time basis in 2008 when it became clear Fidel was not returning. A further five-year term for him was passed in 2013.

Fidel Castro died in November 2016, and Raúl Castro stepped down as the President of Cuba in April 2018. His presidency was marked by significant changes for the island, including opening up a small but crucial private sector, and renewing diplomatic relations with the United States.

Cuba's National Assembly selected a new president, 57-year-old Miguel Díaz-Canel. Raúl (now age 87) had been grooming him for this position for years.

THE FALL OF JUAN PERÓN

Meanwhile, change was afoot in Argentina. Enjoying support from the Church, the military, and the trade unions, Juan Perón had been re-elected for a second term as President in 1952 but unrest quickly began to surface. There were economic problems and the government's relationship with the Catholic Church was eroded.

The Church began to distance itself from Perón which led to confrontation when the government retaliated by removing some of the Church's privileges, forcing the Catholic hierarchy to openly oppose Perón. This influenced the military, and the government's situation was threatened by the formation of a new political entity in Argentina—the Christian Democrat Party.

Anti-government demonstrations broke out and in June 1955, the Argentine Navy and Air Force bombed Plaza de Mayo, a square in Buenos Aires, killing 300 people, launching the *Revolución Libertadora*. It had been targeting the nearby seat of government in front of which a large crowd of Perón supporters had gathered.

Finally on September 16, 1955, Perón was ousted in a military *coup d'état* led by three army generals who formed a provisional government. Fighting broke out during this process and it was the threat of an all-out civil war that persuaded Perón to resign. On September 23, General Lonardi assumed the presidency, promising that once the country was "reorganized," the interim administration would end.

Soon, however, he was replaced by General Aramburu who was more of a hard-liner. Perón's followers were accused of treason, the Perónist party was outlawed, and Perón was exiled. Public references to Perón and his wife were banned. It became so bad that Perón's much loved late wife Evita's remains were covertly moved from Argentina to Italy to protect them from interference.

A CHANCE TO CHANGE THE WORLD

The Argentine exiles in Mexico were delighted to see the back of Juan Perón and the leader of the Radical Civil Union and future President of Argentina, Arturo Frondizi, offered to fly them back home in a plane of the Argentine Navy. Rojo argued with Che about going home, but Che steadfastly refused to go back to Argentina. He undoubtedly still felt unfulfilled and viewed a return to Buenos Aires as a failure.

He saw himself as a revolutionary but at age 27 he had achieved little so far in his life. Admittedly with Perón gone, there may have been opportunities in his homeland, but with no track record there were few prospects the people would take him seriously back in Argentina.

On the other hand, joining forces with the rebels was much more appealing. To the Cubans he was not a footloose bohemian, but a well-educated doctor who shared their views. Revolution in Cuba gave Che exactly what he was looking for—a chance to change the world.

A crowd of several thousand gathered in the Plaza de Mayo, Buenos Aires, Argentina, during the general strike of 1955 to back Juan Perón's campaign against the Roman Catholic Church.

JUAN PERÓN

Juan Domingo Perón (1895 – 1974) was born in Lobos, Buenos Aires province, Argentina. His great-grandfather immigrated to Argentina in the 1830s from Sardinia. Perón was educated at a boarding school run by his maternal grandmother who made sure he received a strict Catholic education.

He enrolled at the National Military College in 1911 at age 16, graduating two years later and commanded an infantry post before being appointed to Army General Staff Headquarters in 1929, when he also married his first wife Aurelia Tizón (1908 – 38). From 1936 to 1938 he was military attaché in the Argentine embassy in Chile but he returned to Argentina to teach in 1938, the same year that his wife died of cancer.

In 1943 he was a leading member of the *coup d'état* that ousted President Ramón Castillo. He was given responsibility for the Ministry of Labor, and increased his popularity in 1944 by helping the victims of the San Juan earthquake. Around this time, he also met his future second wife, the actress Eva "Evita" Duarte (1919 – 52) whom he married in 1945. He was appointed vice president and finally elected as president in 1946.

During his first presidential term (1946 – 52) Perón was supported by Evita, and the couple rode a massive wave of popular support for six years. Evita died from cancer in 1952 at age 33, plunging the country into mourning. She has since become an icon of popular culture, most famously as the subject of the musical *Evita* (1976).

Perón was elected to a second term, serving from 1952 until 1955. He was ousted from the presidency in the *Revolución Libertadora* and went into exile in Venezuela. In 1973 President Hector Cámpara resigned to allow Juan Perón to return and stand for president once more after eighteen years in exile. An estimated three and a half million supporters welcomed him at the airport and he won the election with sixty-two percent of the vote.

He began his third term on October 12, 1973, with his third wife Isabel (born 1931) as his vice president. Nine months later he died after suffering a series of heart attacks, at age 78. Isabel Perón succeeded him as president and remained in office until a military coup in March 1976. Ideologically, the political movement known as Perónism has lived on, and has influenced several subsequent presidents of Argentina.

President Juan Perón and his wife Eva "Evita" Perón wave to the crowds below from the presidential balcony in Buenos Aires, Argentina, 1950.

FULGENCIO BATISTA

Born in Veguita, Cuba, Fulgencio Batista y Zaldívar (1901 – 73) was the son of a man who had fought in the Cuban War of Independence. Batista was of Cuban, Spanish, and Chinese descent. His mother died when he was 14, and he left home for a succession of small time manual jobs. He moved to Havana in 1921 and enlisted in the Cuban Army.

He rose to power during the Sergeants' Revolt in 1933, a coup that brought down the government of Gerardo Machado. Ramón Grau became president, and Batista appointed himself Army Chief of Staff, dominating the new president behind the scenes. Batista forced Grau to resign and went on to control several more short-lived presidencies until he became president himself in 1940. He was the first non-white President of Cuba and was backed by the Communist Party.

In 1944 Batista fled to the United States, claiming he felt safer there. He returned in 1952 and staged a coup with the full support of the Cuban Army. Backed by the US government, Batista abandoned any pretense of progressive politics and set about building up his personal resources.

Wages rose under Batista but the whole country was riddled with corruption. The police operated protection rackets and brothels flourished. In the 1950s Havana became what was described as "a hedonistic playground for the world's elite." The Mafia moved in and set up lucrative gambling, drugs, and prostitution operations. Legend has it that Batista received a thirty percent cut of the profits. Over the years millions of Mafia dollars were deposited in Batista's Swiss bank accounts. After the fall of his government to Castro's rebels in 1959, Batista escaped to the Dominican Republic with a personal fortune believed to be in the region of $300 million.

Denied entry to the United States and Mexico, Batista was finally granted asylum in Portugal. Living in Madeira and then Estoril, he became chairman of a Spanish insurance company. He died in 1973 in Spain, allegedly just two days before a team of Cuban assassins were due to eliminate him. He was 72.

CHAPTER 6

THE CUBAN REVOLUTION

They were ready for revolution, and Castro, using money from well-wishers and supporters, began preparing his revolutionaries for battle to overthrow Fulgencio Batista's dictatorship. To manage the military training of the rebels, Castro turned to a former Spanish Republican Army Officer, the battle-hardened Alberto Bayo.

A REVOLUTIONARY ADVENTURER

Cuban by birth, Alberto Bayo commanded successful guerrilla campaigns during the Spanish Civil War, led the invasion of Ibiza and Majorca, and had been involved with the Caribbean Legion in the 1940s. Castro agreed to pay him 50,000 pesos to run a boot camp for the rebels, but Bayo, a revolutionary adventurer by profession, would have done it for less.

Disguised as an army officer from El Salvador, Bayo rented an abandoned farm named Santa Rosa hidden away about twenty miles outside Mexico City. It was to be their training base where the raw recruits were to be built into a fighting force. Local laborers were hired to work on the farm to simulate normality, while Castro's men secretly trained for an invasion of Cuba.

Bayo put them through a tough, rigorous regime, teaching them all he knew about guerrilla warfare and incorporating the lessons learned from recent conflicts such as the Chinese Civil War. They lived in spartan conditions and rarely left Santa Rosa.

Alberto Bayo transformed Che from a medical doctor into a freedom fighter, and pretty soon he was excelling in everything.

Bayo named him top of the class at the end of the training. Both Bayo and Castro recognized the Argentinean as the best man to lead a campaign of ambushes, sabotage, and hit-and-run tactics, and he was seen as a leader by his fellow trainees. Che never forgot the debt he owed his teacher, writing in a prologue that he provided for Bayo's *My Contribution to the Cuban Revolution*:

> *For me, whom he called his best pupil it is an honor to write these lines as a preface to the memories of a gladiator who is never resigned to being old. Of General Bayo, modern Quixote who fears only that death may not permit him to see his country liberated, I can say that he is my master.*

I WILL NOT ABANDON YOU

By June 22, 1956, the Mexican *Federales* became suspicious of the goings-on at Santa Rosa, raided the farm, and arrested everyone including Che. Not only did it delay the invasion of Cuba, it brought the added threat of extradition for the revolutionaries.

As a non-Cuban, Che felt he was in particular danger of being thrown out of the country and, having pleaded with Castro not to delay the revolution for him, he added that in the event of him being extradited, he would appreciate it if Castro would make efforts to ensure that he was sent anywhere but Argentina. As Che later said, he very much appreciated Castro's reply of "I will not abandon you."

After a month of incarceration, the Mexican authorities responded to moves by Castro

Jungle training, 1957. Fidel Castro and Alberto Bayo stand in the center, with Dr. Ernesto "Che" Guevara second from the left.

supporters in the Mexican government, and the revolutionaries were released. They may also have reasoned that they were really pretty harmless. Their target, after all, was not Mexico but Cuba.

They returned to their training immediately, using various locations in Mexico City now they had lost Santa Rosa. These apartments and houses were later raided by the Mexican police who uncovered guns and ammunition. The interest of the Mexican authorities in the activities of Castro's men forced him to bring forward his plans for the invasion of Cuba before they stopped them altogether.

INVADING CUBA

It was 2:00 a.m. on November 25, 1956, at the Mexican Gulf port of Tuxpán, Veracruz, when the revolutionaries loaded their weapons, supplies, and ammunition onto the yacht *Granma*. The vessel had been purchased for US$15,000 by a Mexican associate thought to have been the arms dealer Antonio "The Friend" del Conde. Eighty-two men of Castro's 26th of July Movement crowded aboard the yacht which was built to hold a maximum of

twenty-five. It was not ideal for an invasion but they could afford nothing better.

Setting off in an overloaded vessel, they were in danger of capsizing at any moment. Soon they left behind the river estuary and hit the open Caribbean Sea where they could at least switch the lights on. The weather was bad, and coastguard authorities had prohibited all navigation that night. Che, as the expedition doctor, was immediately called into action, dealing with seasick revolutionaries. But he himself was in bad shape too, forced to endure an asthma attack that persisted throughout the long voyage.

Onboard, Commander-in-Chief Castro announced the command structure of the expedition. The troops would be led by Captain José Smith, Captain Juan Almeida, and Castro's brother Captain Raúl Castro. Chief of Sanitation was Ernesto "Che" Guevara.

The rebels at the front were given automatic rifles, but Che asked for an old weapon as he thought he would not be of much help. They were each given two uniforms, a backpack, and a pair of boots. Their civilian clothing was thrown into the sea.

GHOSTS AND SHADOWS

The invasion force landed at Niquero on Cuba's southern coast on December 2. Located in the foothills of the Sierra Maestra mountain range, they were finally able to put Bayo's training into practice. Che later described those first hours on Cuban soil:

> *We reached solid ground, lost, stumbling along like so many shadows or ghosts marching in response to some obscure psychic impulse. We had been through seven days of constant hunger and sickness during the sea crossing, topped by three still more terrible days on land. Exactly 10 days after our departure from Mexico, during the early morning hours of December 5, following a night-long march interrupted by fainting and frequent rest periods, we reached a spot paradoxically known as Alegría de Pío (Rejoicing of the Pious).*

In fact, the *Granma* had hit a sandbank a mile offshore and had to be abandoned having run out of fuel. There was further bad luck when the auxiliary boat that was supposed to ferry the weapons to the beach sank when it was lowered into the water.

The men had to carry their weapons ashore and the bulkier equipment had to be left behind. It took two hours to get to dry land where they were then plagued by mosquitoes and gnats. By the time they stopped to rest, many had cuts and lacerations that were in danger of infection. One group of seven men had disappeared altogether.

NO TIME FOR BULLETS

The invaders found a house where the sympathetic owner fed them as the sun came up. But shots could be heard and they discovered that the air force and the coastguards were attacking the swamps where they had landed. The owner of the house led them to a hill where they could hide and await the arrival of the other men.

On the morning of December 5, the revolutionaries were led by another peasant through the sugar cane fields of the New Niquero Sugar Company to Alegría del Pío where they spent the night. But their guide betrayed them, and the Cuban Army now blocked their route to the Sierra Maestra.

Suddenly, shots rang out and someone shouted demanding their surrender. One of the rebels, Camilo Cienfuegos famously replied, *"Aquí no se rinde nadie, carajo!"* (No one surrenders here, Goddamit!). The Army responded by setting fire to the sugar cane fields. It was the moment when Che experienced a symbolic and life-changing predicament, as he later described:

> *A comrade dropped an ammunition box at my feet. I pointed questioningly to it and the man answered me with a face I remember perfectly, for the anguish it reflected seemed to say, "It's no time for bullets," and he immediately left along the path through the cane field (he was later murdered by the Batista forces). This was perhaps the first time I was faced with the dilemma of choosing between my dedication to medicine and my duty as a revolutionary soldier. At my feet were a pack full of medicines and a cartridge box: together, they were too heavy to carry. I chose the cartridge box, leaving behind the medicine pack, and crossed the clearing which separated me from the cane field.*

SURROUNDED BY GUNFIRE

As he ran through the cane field, carrying the box of ammunition, Che was hit in the neck by a bullet and immediately began to lose a lot of blood. He believed the injury was fatal but Juan Almeida checked the wound and announced that it was not life-threatening. Their group managed to cross the field and escape just as it burst into flames. They continued walking and that night huddled together for warmth. Hungry and thirsty, they were being eaten alive by mosquitoes.

Meanwhile, surrounded by gunfire and the sound of searching planes overhead, Castro had withdrawn to a forest with others who had escaped from the burning field. The uniforms and equipment had been abandoned and three of their number had been killed. Many were caught and tortured before being killed. Among these was Che's old friend, Nico López. Of the eighty-two revolutionaries who had boarded the *Granma* in Mexico, there were just twenty men left standing.

TRAVELING BY NIGHT

The various groups headed toward the Sierra Maestra, traveling by night and hoping to meet up with their comrades. Che's group disguised themselves as peasants. They lost all their weapons which was something that made Castro furious when they finally got to him. But Che was quietly pleased to read his own name in a Cuban newspaper listing him as an Argentinean communist, expelled from his own country, fighting for the revolution.

The newspapers also claimed that the Castro brothers and Che had been killed and the revolt had been defeated, causing despair in the Guevara household back in Buenos Aires. Che's farewell letter left with Hilda arrived and heightened the gloom that had descended on the family.

Che's father tried to find out what he could but all he was told was that there was as yet

THE FAVORITE SMOKE

● ● ● ● ● ● ● ● ● ● ● ●

Commercial sale of Cuban cigars has been banned in the US since 1962. Ninety-five percent that are sold in America are fakes as a result of widespread counterfeiting. One of Cuba's leading worldwide exports, Castro's rebels adopted them as a symbol of the revolution.

Che Guevara took up smoking cigars in the jungle, where they suppressed hunger pangs, and the smoke kept the mosquitoes at bay. But they were also good company as Che remarked: "A smoke in times of rest is a great companion to the solitary soldier." They also kept him alert and awake, as he would later find when he worked long hours in his government office.

The distinctive black-and-yellow band of the Cohiba was the favorite smoke of Cuba's revolutionary elite. Soon these long, elegant cigars became as much a part of the revolutionary look as facial hair and military fatigues, thanks to Che Guevara's endorsement that he had never smoked a better cigar.

Che Guevara smoking his favorite Cohiba cigar.

JOSE MARTI

José Julián Martí Pérez (1853 – 95) was born in Havana. His father was a prison guard who had immigrated from Valencia, Spain, and his mother was born in the Canary Islands. When Martí was 4 years old, his family moved back to Valencia but two years later they returned to Cuba. At age 12, he enrolled at the Escuela de Instrucción Primaria Superior Municipal de Varones where he came under the influence of the headmaster Rafael María de Mendive. He went on to Havana Professional School for Painting and Sculpture, initially studying painting but gradually he began to focus on writing. By the age of 16, his poems were being published.

Martí was passionate about efforts to liberate Cuba from Spanish rule and he devoted his literary skills to that cause, establishing the newspaper *La Patria Libre.* His criticism of Spanish rule eventually got him arrested and sentenced to six years hard labor. In 1871 he was released and deported to Spain, where he continued his campaign. He studied law at Zaragoza University, graduating in 1874.

He was allowed to return to Cuba in 1878, but prevented from practicing law by the government. He traveled in Europe and Central America, ending up in New York City where he wrote political articles and literary criticism. His most famous essay, "Our America," written in 1881, called on all Latin American countries to unite.

In 1892, Martí became a member of the Cuban Revolutionary Party and began to plan an invasion of Cuba. He solicited money from Cuban exiles and sympathetic political organizations. On April 11, 1895, they launched their invasion, and Martí was shot dead by Spanish troops.

Martí's life and literature have been an inspiration for many revolutionaries around the world, including Che Guevara and Fidel Castro. He is a national hero of Cuba and is commemorated by a statue in the Plaza de la Revolución in Havana and by having Cuba's José Martí International Airport named in his honor.

no official confirmation of his son's demise. As a last resort he talked with the president's private secretary and President Aramburu took up the case, promising that his Foreign Minister would have investigations carried out in Cuba as to what the real situation was with the rebel band.

SPANISH CATS HAVE SEVEN LIVES

The Guevara family was relieved when a telegram arrived from a cousin of Che's father who happened to be the Argentine ambassador in Havana. "Dr. Ernesto Guevara de la Serna," it read, "according to enquiries made by this embassy, is not among the dead, nor among the wounded, nor among the prisoners of Batista's army." Then, a mysterious envelope appeared under the door one night, as Che's father later wrote:

> It was a small airmail envelope addressed to Celia de la Serna postmarked Manzanillo in Cuba. Inside there was a little piece of paper. It was a page torn from a small notebook and was in handwriting we all knew well. It read, "Dear Viejos: I am fine, I only used up 2 and have 5 still left. I am still doing the same job, news will reach you sporadically and will continue to do so, but trust that God is an Argentine. A big hug to you all. Teté."

The letter was from Che—"Teté" was the nickname known only to the family that he had been given as a baby. Dismissive of the danger, Che joked that he had used up two of his seven Spanish cat lives, but nevertheless he had survived. The Guevara family joyfully celebrated the new year.

LAUNCHING THE ONSLAUGHT

Castro's rebels regrouped on December 24 with fresh arms. They now numbered twenty-two, with new members having joined them. It was time to launch the onslaught. Their target was the small government barracks at the mouth of the La Plata river. A quick hit was essential because, although they had a rifle each, they did not have much spare ammunition. They planned to storm the overseer's house in the compound while two groups attacked the barracks, one from the center, the other from the left.

Castro opened up the night-time assault with a barrage of automatic machine-gun fire while the revolutionaries set the buildings ablaze. The plan worked perfectly. The officers fled quickly and the soldiers who remained behind surrendered. The rebels commandeered eight Springfield rifles, ammunition, backpacks, and clothes. They even took care of the enemy casualties. The attack had claimed the lives of two of them and five more were wounded, but Castro's men escaped without injury. They headed back to the Sierra Maestra with their spirits sky-high after the victory.

THIRSTING FOR BLOOD

The government responded swiftly, dispatching a large taskforce to pin down the rebels inside the Sierra Maestra. They forced the local peasants to tell them where the guerrillas were hiding, throwing them off their land and out of their houses.

Many locals joined Castro to assist in any way they could, but those who chose to betray him were shown no mercy. One such was Eutimo Guerra. Given a summary trial by the revolutionaries, he was sentenced to death on the spot. It is said that it was Che who pulled the trigger with no remorse.

The rebels went on to ambush a government patrol on January 22 at Arroyo del Infierno. They killed five of the patrol before making a getaway back to their hideout. Even though he was suffering from malaria, Che was electrified by their exploits and wrote to Hilda on January 28:

> Here I am in the Cuban jungle, alive and thirsting for blood, writing these fiery lines inspired by Martí as if I were a real soldier (I am dirty and in rags, at least). I write on a field mess-plate with my weapon by my

side and a new addition between my lips: a Havana cigar.

His malaria did not improve and by February he was also suffering from diarrhea. Unable to continue the march, he stopped to rest, two men remained with him until he was well enough to go on. Just as they finally caught up with the rest of their group, the government forces attacked and they all had to flee. Che lost all his medicines, food, blankets, and books, and Julio Zenón, to whom Che had become close, was killed.

THE JUNGLE INTERVIEWS

The rebel profile was boosted when journalist Herbert Matthews from *The New York Times* arrived at their camp on February 17 to interview Castro. Matthews was a veteran war reporter having covered the Spanish Civil War, the Italian War in Abyssinia, and World War II. His interview appeared in numerous newspapers around the world.

Castro deliberately ensured that during the interview, his men continually walked back and forth behind him, giving the impression that his force was much bigger than it actually was. He also arranged for a messenger to arrive from the "Second Column." Of course, there was no Second Column.

Matthews claimed later to have known the game that Castro was playing. The main outcome of the interview, apart from spreading propaganda for Castro's views, was that Batista could no longer deny the existence of the rebels or claim that they had all been wiped out.

The media turned up again on April 23 when a journalist and a cameraman—Bob Taber and Wendell Hoffman—were escorted to the camp. They were covering the insurrection for the American TV network CBS. Their film was broadcast coast to coast on TV screens across the United States. The Cuban Revolution had become very big news indeed.

The rebels of the Sierra Maestra celebrating victory over Batista's government forces.

CHAPTER 7

THE LEGEND IS BORN

Che's duties as a doctor extended far beyond the men with whom he was marching. En route he treated the local people, women old before their time, starving children with distended bellies, people with rickets, and all the ailments that terrible poverty brought to the population. Moreover, he was treating them with a very limited supply of medicines.

Che Guevara in the Sierra Maestra mountains, Cuba, 1957.

THE TOOTHPULLER

He also had to invent new skills as a dentist which earned him a new nickname. As he noted in his diary: "… in the Sierra they gave me the more modest title of 'toothpuller.'" He had no ether to knock the men out while he pulled their teeth, instead using what he described as "psychological anesthesia." This was simply "insulting the man with strong language" whenever there was a complaint about how brutal his technique was.

On May 28, 1957, spirits were lifted when a consignment of guns arrived from Havana. Che was given a repeater rifle, an important moment for him, as he recorded in his diary:

> … I begin to be a direct combatant since so far I have been an occasional one … With this a new stage began for me at the Sierra.

They used these new arms ten days later in a successful attack on the garrison at El Uvero. It was an important victory for them but Che found himself once more caring not just for the wounded on the rebel side but those on the army side too.

June was spent on medical duties and he rejoined the main force at the end of the month, bringing with him new recruits to the cause. Castro promoted him to Captain and he spent his time teaching several of the men to read and write and ran courses on Cuban history and guerrilla warfare. Toward the end of July, he received another promotion, to Comandante and was now entitled to wear a star on his beret. This particular promotion was a complete surprise to him.

The rebel officers had been assembled to sign a letter to Frank País that acknowledged

FRANK PAÍS

Frank País (1934 – 57) was the son of a Protestant pastor and both his parents had immigrated from Galicia in Spain. In 1953, País put together a loose revolutionary group called Revolutionary National Action. This turned into a network of people working toward the downfall of Batista's government. The cells were composed of students and workers with an average age of 17 years. They stashed weapons, repaired them, took part in mass protests, raised money, and collected medical supplies to be used in the revolution.

When Castro's 26th of July Movement began to form, País' organization merged with it and he became the leader of the new group in Oriente Province. The network he had built was far bigger than the police and the authorities thought and to illustrate this fact, País gave instructions for every cell to paint anti-government slogans on walls and buildings throughout Santiago de Cuba. Next morning the people of the city awoke to find slogans scrawled across every spare bit of space.

After Castro and his men landed in Cuba, País organized an insurrection in Santiago de Cuba that lasted four days. He was arrested in March 1957 but there was uproar and he was subsequently released. He then became the organizer of protest and insurrection across the island in support of the rebels fighting in the Sierra Maestra.

The police were coming down hard on rebel sympathizers and País' youngest brother was shot dead by police in June 1957. He was himself forced into hiding but was discovered by the police. He tried to escape with another man but was betrayed by an informant. The two men were taken prisoner and driven to another part of the city where they were executed with a bullet in the back of the head.

Che mourned the loss of a man he called "one of the purest and most glorious" of revolutionaries. In response to his murder, the workers of Santiago de Cuba staged a general strike which was the biggest display of anti-government feeling to-date and a significant moment in the revolution. The day is now known as the Day of the Martyrs of the Revolution. Frank País' childhood home is now a museum and the international airport at Holguín is named after him.

his contribution to the revolutionary struggle. País was Castro's urban commander and an important figure in the Cuban underground movement. When it was Che's turn to sign the letter, he bent over to sign himself as "Captain Che Guevara." But Castro said to him that he should put instead "*Comandante Che Guevara.*"

FIRST CONTACT

Che was now in command of Column No. 4 which was, in reality, only Column No. 2. Castro thought he could keep fooling the enemy into thinking the rebels had more men than they did if he called it the fourth column. Che was extremely proud as Column No. 1 was commanded by Castro himself. So, it was an extraordinary recognition of his contribution and his ability. He was in charge of seventy-five men who were given the task of harassing Cuban Army troops led by Angel Sánchez-Mosquera and Merob Sosa, both of whom had a reputation for brutality and cruelty.

They had their first contact with the enemy on the night of July 31 at Bueyecito but it all went badly wrong. Some units failed to materialize and Che's machine gun jammed,

as did his handgun. This also happened to a companion who was trying to shoot the same sentry. The sentry opened fire on the two hapless rebels and Che unashamedly took to his heels. By the time he made his weapon operational again, it was all over. The garrison had surrendered to another rebel unit, led by Ramiro Valdés. Frustrated, Che tossed away his Thompson submachine gun, replacing it with a Browning that he had grabbed from the garrison.

THE MASTER TACTICIAN

On August 29, Che's column saw action again at El Hombrito. They waited by the road at a point where a column of enemy troops had to turn a corner around a rock. Che planned to let ten or so soldiers pass before opening fire, separating these ten men from the remainder of the troops. They would then gun down the soldiers and force the column to retreat. In reality, Che opened fire after just six men had passed, having heard a shout and in the end, just one of the six was shot, the others managed to flee. Che was disappointed and said that:

Fidel Castro (standing) planning tactics with Che Guevara (left) during the revolution.

> *[the operation] proved to us the inadequate combat preparation of our troop, which was incapable of firing accurately upon enemies who were moving such a short distance away as in this battle, where there could not have been more than 10 or 20 meters between the head of the enemy column and our positions.*

Their classic guerrilla tactics were very effective, however, as the conflict continued:

> *This battle showed us how easy it was, under certain circumstances, to attack enemy columns on the march. Besides, it convinced us of the correctness of the tactical excellence of always firing at the head of the column on the march in order to try to kill the first man, or first men, thus ensuring that the others do not move forward and so immobilizing the enemy force. This tactic was perfected little by little, finally being carried out so systematically that the foe stopped penetrating the Sierra Maestra and produced a scandal, for the soldiers refused to join the vanguard.*

Numerous engagements with enemy troops followed at Mar Verde, Minas del Frio, Las Mercedes, Vegas de Jibocoa, and three at Pino del Agua. Che fought in all of them, but the most important campaign he waged was the final one which was fought at Las Villas Province, now Villa Clara Province, in the island's central region. It was this campaign that turned Che into the greatest leader of the Cuban Revolution and established his reputation as a master tactician of guerrilla warfare.

THE FINAL CAMPAIGN

The strategy for the final campaign, as determined by Castro was a simple one. It was very much based on the victorious strategy that the leaders of Cuba's War of Independence had implemented in 1896. The rebels' first column, named "José Martí" and commanded by Castro, stayed in Oriente. Column 6, the "Frank País" Column, of which Raúl Castro was in charge would also stay there.

They were loosely encircling Santiago while

Column 2, "Antonio Maceo" led by Camilo Cienfuegos, marched westward toward the province of Pinar del Río at the other end of the island. Column 8, commanded by Che and named after Ciro Redondo, one of the rebels who had recently lost his life, was ordered to make for Las Villas Province. Castro described Che's objectives in an order he issued on August 21, 1958:

> *Column 8 "Ciro Redondo" will leave Las Mercedes between August 24 and 30. Comandante Ernesto Guevara is named chief of the Rebel units of the July 26th Movement operating in the Province of Las Villas, in the rural as well as the urban zones, and is granted powers to collect and disburse for war purposes taxes levied according to our military requirements; to apply the Penal*

Che Guevara (left) and Fidel Castro (right) in the Sierra Maestra mountains, Cuba, 1958.

Code and Agrarian Laws of the Rebel Army in the territory where his forces operate; to coordinate operations, plans, administrative functions, and military organization with other revolutionary forces which operate in the province, which should be invited to integrate into one single Army Corps in order to strengthen and unify the Revolution; to organize local combat units and appoint Rebel Army officers up to the rank of column commander. Column 8 will have the strategic objective of pounding away unceasingly at the enemy in the central territory of Cuba, and of intercepting, until they are totally paralyzed, the movements of enemy troops by land from west to east.

The ultimate aim was to split the island in two, severing communications between each part.

THE PERILOUS PLAN OF ATTACK

Alerted that another supply of ammunition was arriving on a DC-3 transport plane at Manzanillo, on the Gulf of Guacanayabo, Che set off with 150 hand-picked men to get it, before heading to Las Villas. They were armed with the best weapons the rebels had—Springfield rifles, Garand semi-automatic rifles, M1-carbines, a couple of .30 caliber machine guns, two Brownings, two Berettas, and a bazooka. They boarded trucks with enough supplies for what Che thought would be a four-day journey to Las Villas.

But government troops spotted the DC-3 landing at Manzanillo, and pounded the airfield for several hours with artillery fire. By dawn the next day, Che decided they had to blow up the plane full of ammunition rather than let it fall into enemy hands. The problem was it would starve them of ammunition and might also bring an abrupt end to their mission before they had even begun. In addition the vehicle bringing gas supplies for the trucks had been intercepted rendering the trucks useless. But Che was determined to carry out Castro's perilous plan of attack. They would have to make the journey on foot.

They set off on August 31, almost immediately encountering rugged terrain, terrible weather, and many impossible rivers to cross. They had very little food and water and were victim to swarms of mosquitoes. At the same time, they were being pursued and surrounded by Batista's troops and aircraft.

Che led by example, rejecting any preferential treatment, his boots just as in need of repair as everyone else's. He constantly made sure their equipment was all working perfectly, so guns would not jam in battle, and that guards remained vigilant defending the camp. While his men slept, he prowled the camp double-checking for himself that no work was only half-done or below his own exacting standards.

The rebels finally escaped the encirclement and, with the enemy still in hot pursuit, they swam across the Júcaro River to Las Villas. They had taken seven weeks to get there instead of four days, and it was now October 6, 1958.

The Sierra Maestra rebels on a jungle march, 1958.

CAMILO CIENFUEGOS

Born in Havana, Camilo Cienfuegos Gorriarán (1932 – 59) was one of Fidel Castro's top commanders and was known as the "Hero of Yaguajay" after winning a key battle of that name. One historian has described him as exemplifying "the quintessential native, male, urban Cuban with his sense of humor, great interest in dancing, and baseball, good looks, love of women, and overall *joie de vivre*." He is a hero of the revolution with many statues, monuments, and memorials built in his honor.

His working-class family had emigrated from Spain before the Spanish Civil War. Showing artistic talent from an early age, Cienfuegos whose name translates into "a hundred fires" in English, enrolled at the Escuela Nacional de Bellas Artes "San Alejandro" in 1950, the oldest and most prestigious art school in Cuba. Unfortunately, he could not afford to remain there and left soon after, starting work as an apprentice tailor in a fashion shop in Havana.

In 1953 Cienfuegos traveled with a friend to the United States where they worked illegally in San Francisco, New York City, and Chicago,

eventually being deported by US Immigration to Cuba. In 1954 Cienfuegos became a member of a Cuban student underground movement that was working to bring down President Batista.

Harassed by the authorities for his political activities, Cienfuegos left Cuba for the United States again in March 1956 before traveling south to Mexico where he joined up with Fidel Castro, and was one of the eighty-two who made the fateful voyage on the *Granma*. He differed from the others in many ways. Not as politically extreme as Castro or Che, he did not believe in violence and revenge. When Castro came to power, Cienfuegos was appointed Chief of Staff of the Cuban Army.

On October 28, 1959, a small plane carrying Cienfuegos vanished over the Straits of Florida. The wreckage was never found, and Cienfuegos was reported lost at sea presumed dead. He was 27 years old. Many conspiracy theories surrounded his death including one that Fidel Castro himself was responsible, but his disappearance remains unexplained to this day.

Camilo Cienfuegos (left) and Che Guevara in Ha

THE OVERTHROW OF BATISTA

Their first task was to stop the elections planned for November 3. Batista had finally relented amid the clamor for his resignation and agreed to step down. But, fearing the installation of a Batista puppet as president, Castro and other anti-Batista elements had called for a nationwide boycott of the election. Unfortunately, Che's delay in arriving in the province prevented him influencing the election but such was the success of the anti-Batista boycott and so great was the hatred for the dictator that the turnout was very low, in any case.

The next step was to close the roads. Che and his men blocked the important route from Trinidad to Sancti Spíritus, closed the bridge over the Tuinicú River, and blocked railway lines. They were helped by the Second National Front of Escambray which was another guerrilla force affiliated to the Directorio Revolucionario Estudantil (the Revolutionary Student Directorate). Revolutionary Camilo Cienfuegos was also cutting railway lines in the north of the province.

By the middle of December, Che had closed even more roads and bridges. On December 16 he and his men blew up the vital bridge over the Rio Falcón on the main road, the Central Highway. This severed communications between Havana and the cities and towns of the east of the island. Batista now had to use planes to supply his troops in Santiago, an expensive and difficult method.

On December 21, in a concerted effort, Che and Cienfuegos columns launched attacks on towns and villages. Che hit the strategically important points of Cabaiguán and Guayos, to cut the Central Highway completely, while Cienfuegos struck at villages in the north, throwing a cordon round the town of Yaguajay in the province of Sancti Spiritus. Cienfuegos had started out with just sixty men, but by the time he reached Santa Clara he had around 500 troops under his command, many locals joining his forces along the road to revolution.

Cuban revolutionaries attacking a Nationalist Army post during the Battle of Santa Clara, Cuba, December 1958.

The wreckage at Santa Clara after Che's rebel forces blew up and derailed the train carrying Batista's troops.

CAPTURING SANTA CLARA

Santa Clara was a city of 150,000 inhabitants, by far the biggest city the rebels had tried to capture. It was in the heart of Cuba, located in the very center of the island and was a hub for railway and road traffic. On December 29, the Battle of Santa Clara began. Che established a base at the university while Batista dispatched an armored train carrying four hundred soldiers to defend the city.

But they were no match for the mobile hit-and-run tactics of the rebels who pinned down the government troops as they tried to defend the train. Eventually, the troops tried to retreat by rail but the rebels had already blown up the tracks and the train derailed. Tossing Molotov cocktails at the beleaguered troops, the rebels forced them from the train as it began to burn ferociously. Within a few hours they had surrendered, leaving Che and his men with a fantastic array of munitions, anti-aircraft guns, and machine guns.

Santa Clara fell into rebel hands on the first day of 1959, the most startling victory of the war so far. It was the pivotal moment in the conflict because Fulgencio Batista immediately resigned the presidency and fled to Trujillo's Dominican Republic. His officials followed him, together with senior officers of the Cuban Army, Air Force, and Navy. Police officers and politicians who were closely associated with him and his government also left the country.

Batista was gone and Cuba was Castro's. On January 2, Ernesto "Che" Guevara, one-time Argentinean adventurer and hobo, marched into Havana at the head of his victorious troops, a Cuban hero who had freed the nation from tyranny and brought triumph to the Cuban Revolution. The legend was born.

Che makes a rousing speech from the top of a jeep congratulating and exhorting the rebels onward to victory at Santa Clara, Cuba, December 1958.

PART THREE

THE CUBAN CONQUEST

THEY MAY KILL THE REVOLUTIONARY,
BUT NEVER THE REVOLUTION.
CHE GUEVARA

CHAPTER 8

JUSTICE IN HAVANA

It was the end of a very profitable era for the Mafia in Cuba. Mob bosses such as Meyer Lansky, "Lucky" Luciano, Bugsy Siegel, and Santo Trafficante had made millions through gambling and prostitution during the Batista years. Now they all made a swift exit, either by air or in their luxury yachts. While they had jetted in and out of Havana's airport to cavort in the casinos, bars, and brothels of the capital, the Cuban population had been underfed, illiterate, and had a life expectancy of only thirty years.

THE MESSENGER OF LOVE

The new mission given to Che and his men was to take the massive fortress of La Cabaña in Havana. Che gave a speech of thanks to the people of Las Villas and with his ranks bolstered by new recruits, hit the road for the capital. He was himself injured, having broken a bone in his arm while climbing a parapet, and his right arm was in plaster. It was held close to his body with a black gauze scarf from which Aleida March had fashioned a sling.

Aleida had been a messenger for Castro's troops and had brought a large sum of cash to them when they were in the Sierra Maestra. It became too dangerous for her to leave, so she remained with them, as a member of Che's force. While the pair were left alone in a jeep during a refueling stop, Che confessed to her that he was in love with her. Aleida apparently said nothing in reply, partly because she was so tired, partly because she thought she had misheard him, but mostly because she was so in awe of him.

Che and his troops arrived in Havana on January 2, 1959, and immediately occupied the fortress of La Cabaña. Some government troops were still billeted there and Che demanded his men live side by side with them without any trouble. He seized the commandant's house located in the fortress's grounds, and gave Aleida March the apartment next to his, which raised a few eyebrows.

Che in Havana, Cuba, photographed by Osvaldo Salas in 1959.

ALEIDA MARCH

Aleida March de la Torre was born in 1936 in Santa Clara, Cuba. She had been delivering messages to Castro's men when they were in the Sierra Maestra but her role was discovered by the authorities and it became too dangerous for her to continue. So she stayed with the rebels and was an active combatant in Che Guevara's Column 8 that marched on her home town.

Apparently, Che was initially reluctant to have a pretty girl in his column because he feared that she would be a distraction. But she was conscientious and hard-working. In the end, he even gave her a weapon. During the fighting around Santa Clara, Che fell in love with her, confessing his feelings to her en route to Havana.

He divorced his first wife Hilda on June 2, 1959, and married Aleida on the same day in the fortress of La Cabaña in Havana. The couple had four children and she wrote a book— *Remembering Che: My Life with Che Guevara* (2008)—about her relationship with Che and how she managed to bring up their four children after his death.

Che and Aleida March leaving for their honeymoon, June 3, 1959, with bodyguards in the rear seat of the car.

LA CABAÑA

• • • • • • • • • •

Its full name is Fortaleza de San Carlos de la Cabaña, but it is popularly known simply as La Cabaña. Situated on a hill on the eastern bank of the entrance to the harbor in Havana, it is an eighteenth-century structure which is the third-largest fortress complex in the Americas. It stands alongside the Morro Castle which dates back to 1592.

La Cabaña was built by the Spanish to improve the defense of Havana after its capture by the British and subsequent return to Spanish control in exchange for Florida. King Carlos III of Spain ordered construction of the fortress in 1763. By the time it was completed in 1774, it was the second-largest colonial military installation in the New World, beaten only by the fortification of St. Felipe de Barajas at Cartagena in Colombia, also built by the Spanish.

For 200 years, the fortress was an important base for Spain and for Cuba once it had gained independence. It was captured by the troops of the Cuban Revolution in January 1959, the Cuban Army defending force offering no resistance, and La Cabaña became Che's headquarters.

It was a military prison for the first few months after the rebels took control, and within the fortress, Che oversaw military tribunals and executions of war criminals and political prisoners. Many members of Batista's Buró para Represión de las Actividades Comunistas were executed or simply disappeared during this time.

The lighthouse of La Cabaña Fort, Havana, Cuba.

THE ULTIMATE TRIUMPH

Castro had been touring Cuba triumphantly for a week before arriving in Havana on January 8. He beamed from the top of a tank or from an open-topped jeep on television screens, the news covering his progress every step of the way. At Matanzas he was met by Che and Aleida who had driven out to greet him before the ultimate triumphant entry into Havana.

After entering the city, Castro delivered a lengthy speech at Camp Columbia, detailing the years of struggle that had preceded the revolution and outlining his plans for the future. At one of the speech's pivotal moments, a dove suddenly landed on his shoulder while two others fluttered around the stage. There have been many theories about these doves, one being that they had been trained to perform in this way. Whatever the truth, it was indeed an inspirational moment.

Hundreds of thousands of delighted Cubans watched it live while millions followed it on the television news or saw it on the front pages of their newspapers. It was the first of many such long speeches by Castro, a tactic he called "direct democracy" because during them he would seek approval for policy decisions or ask for the people's opinion. It was a type of consultation in lieu of elections.

On the day after Castro's speech in Havana, Camilo Cienfuegos sprang a wonderful surprise on Che. His parents and younger brother Juan Martín as well as his sister Celia and her husband turned up, having been flown to Cuba by Cienfuegos on a plane that had been sent to collect Cuban exiles. Che had not seen his family since he set off with Carlos Ferrer in 1953, almost six years previously, when he was 25. At that time, he had nothing to his name except his doctor's qualification and some books. Now he was 30 years old and had helped create a revolution that had changed a nation.

Fidel Castro raises his arm in triumph, as he enters Havana with his bodyguards, January 1959.

CASTRO'S COMMANDERS

Standing left to right: Raúl Castro, Antonio Núñez Jiménez, Che Guevara, Juan Almeida, and Ramiro Valdés in Havana during the first year of the Cuban revolution.

Che Guevara, Manuel Urrutia, and Camilo Cienfuegos during the celebration of Castro's rebel victory.

THE FIRST PRESIDENT

The 26th of July Movement chose Manuel Urrutia (1901 – 81) as the revolutionary government's first president. He returned from exile in Venezuela, having been a prominent member of the anti-Batista movement during the last few years. He was a Christian and an educated liberal, and thought by the leaders of the revolution to be a choice that would pacify the Americans.

Urrutia immediately began to close the brothels and casinos as well as the national lottery, to his mind, all corrupting influences. Of course, this was disastrous for the many thousands employed in these operations and Castro was forced to stop Urrutia's closures until the employees could be found alternative employment.

The president and Castro also disagreed about pay cuts that Castro wanted to impose on public officials, including a cut of $100,000 on Urrutia's own wage. By February 1959, Castro had taken on the role of prime minister, replacing Urrutia's choice, José Miró who resigned after being in office just six weeks.

Castro's prominence in the government seriously reduced Urrutia to little more than a figurehead. But he continued to disagree with Castro on fundamental issues such as elections. Urrutia wanted to introduce them, but Castro thought they would only take Cuba back to the previous corrupt system.

The newspaper *Avance* printed a story when Urrutia bought a luxury villa, which looked to Cubans like a return to the bad old days of Batista and led to accusations of a betrayal of the Revolution. Meanwhile, Urrutia became openly critical of communist elements within the government, having been against the communists ever since they refused to support his fight against the Batista regime.

Castro denounced Urrutia on television, berating him for his fervent anti-communism, and the leader of the sugar workers union demanded the president's resignation. There was uproar as crowds gathered outside the presidential palace. Finally on July 17, 1959, Urrutia resigned, seven months after taking office. Castro duly appointed Osvaldo Dorticós in his place, hoping for a better outcome.

PASSING JUDGEMENT

Meanwhile, Che set up the Military Cultural Academy at La Cabaña and established a new newspaper, *La Cabaña Libre*. Classes were provided for all rebels who wanted to learn to read and write, and there were also lessons on geography, history, economics, and world politics.

Everyone had to attend classes involving military matters and mechanics, and there were leisure and sporting activities. A mass wedding ceremony was held for all guerrillas who were in a relationship. Che delivered a speech—his first since victory—when he was granted an honorary doctorate by the Havana Medical School.

Despite his relationship with Aleida, Che was already married to Hilda Gadea and was the father of a daughter with her. Hilda arrived in Havana on January 21, and it seemed right that she should be there. She had, after all, been generous to Che in Guatemala and Mexico when he had nothing. On her return to her home town of Lima, she had continued working for Castro's 26th of July Movement. Che was also anxious to re-introduce himself to his daughter Hildita whom he had not seen for so long.

There were other personal matters to be dealt with too. Even before he had met Aleida, in Che's mind his marriage with Hilda was over and he had declared this in a letter to his parents while he was in the guerrilla training camp in Mexico. So, as ever going straight to the point, he informed Hilda soon after her arrival that he loved someone else and wanted a divorce.

In late January, Che met with the Chilean politician and future president, Dr. Salvador Allende at La Cabaña. But his real work began in February when he created a tribunal for "the enemies of the Cuban people," passing judgment on those who had tortured, extorted, and killed during the Batista years.

PROOF IS SECONDARY

Che's behavior and his actions during this period have been the subject of much debate. He had the last word on the fate of the many people who were charged and is accused of administering summary justice. Those who are opposed to Castro's revolution have claimed that he sent thousands to their deaths but the number would appear to be closer to two hundred. It seems impossible to equate the monster described by some with the educated, cultured individual who, at the time, was in a loving relationship and had a great deal of rewarding work ahead of him. At the same time, hard-line words are said to have constantly crossed his lips: "It is not possible to tolerate even the suspicion of treason" and "We do not need to use bourgeois legal methods—the proof is secondary."

The memorial march in Havana on March 5, 1960, for the victims of the *La Coubre* freight ship explosion. (Left to right) Fidel Castro, President Osvaldo Dorticós, Che Guevara, Camilo Cienfuegos, and Antonio Núñez Jiménez.

After all, it was his job to perpetuate the revolution, and to make sure that the enemy was destroyed once and for all so they could not regroup to form a resistance movement. He did not forget the lessons he had learned from the Guatemalan Revolution when the Army betrayed Arbenz. He wanted to crush the Cuban Army, as he wrote in *Guerrilla Warfare: A Method*:

> It is necessary to think of destroying the oppressor army. There was also a fear that the people, baying for revenge against those who had repressed them all those years, might take the law into their own hands. The new administration, therefore, decided to deal with the situation and if that meant summary justice and trial without a jury, then so be it.

THE EXECUTION ORDER

Che was not the only rebel leader acting in this way. Raúl Castro is reported to have dispatched seventy-one pro-Batista supporters in one bloody day—January 13, 1959. *The New York Times* correspondent Ruby Hart Phillips described the justice being dispensed at the military trials:

> One night Ted [correspondent Edward Scott] and I went over to see one of the military trials, which were usually held at night. In one of the courtrooms opposite the headquarters building, a man was on trial for his life. The three judges sat at a table on a platform. Just below was the prisoner guarded by two soldiers. It was a dismal scene. The masonry walls were peeling, the chairs were wobbly and there was only a dim light … A couple of witnesses testified that the prisoner had betrayed a revolutionary to the Batista authorities. The judges sent out for Coca-Cola … There were no defense witnesses. The defense attorney made no defense but apologized to the court for defending the prisoner. The whole procedure was sickening. Ted and I left around 11:00 p.m. We learned that half an hour later the prisoner was ordered executed … [he] was shot at two in the morning.

UNTIL JUSTICE IS DONE

The trials were held in public and in one spectacular instance 17,000 came to watch as Major Jesus Sosa Blanco was sentenced at a huge sports palace built at great expense by Batista. Che did not personally attend the hearings, preferring to review each case in the evening with the relevant judge but it seems that he believed that the best way to protect the revolution was by using a firing squad to eliminate any potential future dangers. He had developed into a merciless military man, toughened by the relentless warfare he had witnessed during his years in the Sierra Maestra.

This ruthless side of Che was very familiar to his soldiers with whom he had been a tough disciplinarian, willing to fire a bullet into the temple of anyone who betrayed the principles of the Revolution or who was not doing his job properly. He demonstrated that brutal side of his character in a story he wrote in his book *Pasajes*:

> I had admonished a soldier for sleeping at the height of battle and he replied that he had been disarmed because he had fired a shot accidentally. I replied with my habitual dryness: "Get yourself another rifle by going to the front disarmed as you are … if you have the guts." While lending a word of encouragement to the wounded in the Hospital de Sangre, in Santa Clara, a dying man touched my hand and said, "Remember, Comandante? You sent me to find a gun in Remedios … and I got me one, here." He was the soldier who had fired off accidentally, and who minutes later died, and he seemed to me content to have demonstrated his courage. So was our Rebel Army.

An outside world initially sympathetic to the glamorous revolutionaries was appalled at the violent executions, but Castro was defiant, insisting: "They will go on, until justice has been done."

ALBERTO KORDA

Alberto Korda (1928 – 2001) was the Cuban photographer responsible for taking the iconic photograph of Che Guevara known as *Guerrillero Heroico* that has become the most reproduced photograph in the history of the camera.

Korda, who was born Alberto Díaz Gutiérrez in Havana, launched his first studio, Studios Korda, in 1953 with fellow photographer Luis Pierce (1912 – 85), specializing in fashion and advertising. Soon Alberto Korda was Cuba's best known fashion photographer although he later confessed that his main aim was to meet glamorous women. He became Fidel Castro's official photographer and effectively the photographer of the revolution, traveling with Castro on foreign trips and back to the Sierra Maestra in 1959.

In March 1960, the revolutionaries attended the memorial service in Havana for the victims of *La Coubre* explosion. Korda was taking pictures of the solemn occasion and he took two quick snaps of a grieving and angry Che as he walked across his field of vision. It was certainly a powerful image. Korda did not know it at the time, but he had just taken what would later be called "the most famous photograph in the world." He enlarged it and hung it on his wall.

In 1967 he passed it to Italian publisher Giangiacomo Feltrinelli who was about to publish Che's Bolivian Diary and was searching for a suitable cover image. Korda gave the image to him for free and Feltrinelli made a poster from the photo, distributing thousands of copies around Cuba.

Korda was never credited, but his photo was everywhere in the ensuing decades. By the end of the 1960s, the charismatic image had helped transform Che into a cultural icon. Korda said if he had been given a lira for each reproduction, he would have made millions. However, Alberto Korda died of a heart attack in 2001 at age 73, never having made a cent out of one of the most famous photos of the twentieth century.

GUERRILLERO HEROICO

The iconic photograph of Che Guevara, at age 31, was taken by Alberto Korda on March 5, 1960, at the memorial service for the victims of the *La Coubre* explosion in Havana. The photographer snapped two quick shots of the revolutionary leader as he walked momentarily across his camera lens before disappearing into the crowd. Che's facial expression was a stoic mixture of anger and pain. Korda later said: "I remember it as if it were today ... seeing him framed in the viewfinder, with that expression. I am still startled by the impact ... it shakes me so powerfully." The original photo shown here captured Che between an anonymous silhouette of a man and some palm leaves, artifacts that were cropped out of the final version.

CHAPTER 9

THE POWER BEHIND CASTRO

Given his remarkable contribution to Cuban history, it was very appropriate that Che was granted Cuban citizenship. He was now 31 years old, world-famous, and second in the Cuban hierarchy behind Castro, higher in the chain of command even than Raúl Castro. He had achieved it by virtue of his intelligence, his quick wits, his leadership skills, and the extraordinary courage he demonstrated on the field of battle. He was described at this time by Ruby Hart Phillips of *The New York Times* as:

> a slim dark man ... He wore his brown, slightly curly hair to his shoulders. His eyes were cold and gave an Asiatic cast to his features ... He was soft-spoken, quiet in manner and had none of the hearty comradeship which Fidel Castro displayed.

THE BASIS OF ALL EVIL

The Rebel Army had only ever dreamed of being so firmly in charge, and no one quite knew what the next step should be. With no clear political stance coming from Castro, it was Che who took the country in the direction of communism. If Cuba is today one of the few communist states left in the world it is due to his actions and philosophy at that time.

On January 27, in a speech on the anniversary of the birth of José Martí, he outlined a revolutionary program for Cubans. He wanted Cuba to become an "armed democracy," a notion straight out of Russian communist revolutionary Vladimir Lenin's philosophy. Every Cuban should belong to the Rebel Army.

He denounced the large estates of Cuba (the *latifundios*) as "the basis of all [Cuba's]

economic evils," and demanded they be nationalized. He called for agrarian reform and the abolition of the land-ownership system operating in Cuba at the time. He insisted on the nationalization of Cuba's mineral resources and its privately owned telephone system.

He went on to describe his theory of revolution for the whole of the American continent, a belief that he had espoused since he was a very young man. It could be done, he said, using the model the Cuban Revolution had created:

> We have demonstrated that a small group of determined men, helped by the people and without fear of dying if necessary, can assert itself against a disciplined regular army and defeat it decisively. That is the fundamental lesson. There is another that our brothers elsewhere in America must grasp ... The revolution is not limited to the Cuban nation ... let this be the first step toward the victory of America.

ECONOMIST OR COMMUNIST?

From the tribunals at La Cabaña, Che moved on to the Instituto Nacional de Reforma Agraria, an institution he had created to promote the new agrarian law. He ran the important Department of Industries in this critical and influential body. He lasted just seven weeks there, however, suddenly becoming the President of the Banco Nacional de Cuba.

It has been said that during one of the regular meetings of the revolutionary leaders, Castro announced that he needed a replacement for the prominent economist Felipe Pazos who had held the post, asking, "Is there an economist in the room?" Che thought Castro had asked "Is there a communist in the room?" and immediately volunteered.

"Communist," he answered, "Why, of course! Me!" As a result of this misheard word, he was appointed to this key position, and although Che was many things, he certainly was not an economist.

Pazos had resigned along with other cabinet members because he objected to the threats to execute Comandante Huber Matos, a hero of the Revolution. Matos had opposed the government's move toward Marxist principles and its ties to Cuba's Communist Party. As it was, Matos was instead sentenced to twenty years in prison and lived to the ripe old age of 95, but the resignation of the ministers and the appointment of a communist to run Cuba's national bank spelled the end to any doubts about the political direction in which the island was moving.

BACKING THE USSR

Che's appointment created the immediate consequence of a run on the banks, and he instantly tried to reassure the public, although the truth was that he did not like money and the capitalist system it engendered. He showed his disdain and angered many when the signature that he used on Cuban banknotes read simply "Che."

For the time being he had to make efforts to stabilize the nation's financial system. His power was somewhat constrained, however, as national economic policy did not lie in his hands alone although he did wield some influence on economic decisions.

His greatest achievement at this time was a trade pact negotiated with the Soviet Union. It was concluded during a visit to Cuba in February 1960 by the Soviet politician Anastas I. Mikoyan. The arrangement was basically for the Russians to purchase a million tons of Cuban sugar every year from 1961 to 1965 with a further increase after the initial years. In return, Cuba would back the USSR at the United Nations by supporting her "peaceful coexistence" policy toward capitalist nations.

Fidel Castro meeting Soviet politician Anastas Mikoyan, Havana, Cuba, 1960.

FEELING INVULNERABLE

It was a significant moment, signaling Cuba's shift toward the Soviet sphere of influence. Later this would turn into a dependence on the Russians and it could be argued that Che's deal eroded Cuban independence, contrary to all that he believed in.

He was adamant that national independence was key, especially for underdeveloped countries such as Cuba. The deal also heralded a move away from the United States, but America was refusing to have dealings with the Cuban revolutionary government anyway. Therefore to some extent, Cuba had little choice but to create a partnership with the Soviet Union, unequal though it would prove to be.

Che now felt invulnerable with the power of the Soviet Union behind him. He felt that it would negate any measures taken by the United States to punish the island for developing a socialist agenda on America's doorstep.

SUGAR DEPENDENCY

In February 1960, he established the Central Planning Board (popularly known as Juceplan) whose job was to lay down Cuban economic policy. It had five members, of whom Che was one and it gave him direct access to the formulation of the country's economic policy.

Shortly after its establishment, Che declared that the government was going to nationalize five industries, taking shares of anything between 51 and 100 percent in them. Foreigners and foreign companies were prohibited from investing in these industries among which was the island's most important industry—sugar.

His principal objective was diversification of the Cuban economy. He sought to move it from its complete dependence on sugar. This would remove the power over Cuba that the United States had through the sugar quota that brought in about $150 million a year. The Soviet Union would have to fill that gap. As Che told the Cubans, the Americans used this quota to "enslave" Cubans.

Meanwhile, in his personal life, Aleida gave birth to their first child, a daughter. Che was in Peking at the time but on his return to Havana he and his wife chose the name Aleida for her, although he always called her Aliusha.

Harvesting of sugar cane in Cuba, 1960.

INCREASING ISOLATION

On January 3, 1961, the United States broke off diplomatic relations with Cuba, cutting off the island entirely from its massive neighbor. There could be no diplomacy between the two, no trade, and no travel. Peru, staunchly loyal to the USA, was next. Other Latin American countries added to Cuba's isolation in its region, for a variety of reasons.

Some, like Peru, wanted to do as Washington demanded, other regimes had to because they were supported by the USA, and some who had seized power by illegal means hoped that by supporting the American stance on Cuba, the Americans would give their government legitimacy. It was little surprise that Paraguay broke off relations, ruled as it had been since 1954 by General Alfredo Stroessner, a right-wing dictator whose lengthy term in office (until 1989) would be beaten only by that of Castro himself.

President John F. Kennedy had taken office in January 1961 and the CIA was now beginning to become actively involved in anti-Cuban activities. They had established a Center for Cuban Studies that created disinformation intended to make Cuba look bad to the rest of the world, portraying the Revolution as a failure. Its aim was to undermine and engineer the downfall of the Cuban revolutionary government.

NATIONALIZATION

In March 1961, Che declared economic war on the USA with full-scale nationalization. Between June 29 and July 1, Cuba nationalized the three US oil refineries—Texaco, Esso, and Shell. They had refused to refine Soviet oil and received no compensation for their lost facilities. The Americans responded in July by suspending the sugar quota of around 700,000 tons due to be purchased from Cuba that year.

Che then launched a program of rapid industrialization, reducing the production of sugar to achieve the diversification of the economy he sought. But it resulted in chaos and failed miserably, putting Che at odds with the communists of the Popular Socialist Party and also with his friends, the Soviet Union.

The program of nationalization, however, was swift and between August 6 and October 25 the Cuban government took possession of every American business and plantation. It is estimated that the value of these seizures was around $1.5 billion. The first fortnight in October saw the nationalization of some 382 companies owned predominantly by Cubans. Almost every bit of Cuban industry was now owned by the Cuban government.

But such a swift nationalization had consequences, and there were shortages and inflation. Che, meanwhile was claiming that it was more important to create workers' clubs, open crèches, and children's homes:

Communist Cuban banknotes were introduced in 1961. The images in the design highlighted the revolutionary struggle to establish the regime.

> *We are building thousands of homes, although we know from a purely economic point of view it would be better to build factories.*

Prophetic words indeed. Without the factories it would soon become impossible to achieve all the other plans Che had.

STAYING LOYAL TO RUSSIA

Che was relying on his trade deals with the Soviet Union to bring in the foreign exchange that would enable Cuba to import capital and consumer goods. To this end, he signed further trade agreements with other members of the Soviet bloc. He also concluded agreements with Communist China, the Chinese agreeing to purchase annually 500,000 tons of Cuban sugar. The amount would later be increased in the same way as in the deal with the Russians.

The Chinese and Soviet Union seemed to be vying with each other for Cuba's favor but Che was extra careful around this time to remain loyal to the Russians, even though he was fascinated by Maoism. He made deals with East Germany, traveling there in December, where he met for the first time Tamara Bunke

Bider who would become known as "Tania the Guerrilla," and would later figure in his life. Another treaty with the Russians promised that they would build a hundred new factories in Cuba.

GLOBAL STATESMAN

Che left Cuba for the first time after the Revolution in June 1959, not long after his marriage to Aleida. The summer was spent visiting Egypt, India, Japan, Indonesia, Pakistan, and Communist Yugoslavia. It is said that Castro ordered him to go, perhaps to bring a temporary halt to his push to the left. Castro was concerned that Che was moving too fast.

They also wanted to find out how the world viewed revolutionary Cuba and if they had any chance of aid from these countries, especially from the Communist countries. But although Castro might have been anxious about Che's agenda, he was happy to let him carry on with his nationalization initiatives. It was evidence of Che's growing importance and his influence over Castro and Cuba.

United Arab Republic President Nasser (right) meets with Che at the presidential palace in Cairo, Egypt, 1959, during Che's tour of the Middle East as the head of the Cuban Economics Commission.

CUBA BEFORE THE REVOLUTION

• • • • • • • • • •

At the start of the eighteenth century, the sale of sugar to the United States made Cuba a wealthy country although income inequality was very high and much of the wealth fell into the hands of foreign investors. Before the revolution, per capita income in Cuba was the fifth highest in the region, it was third in life expectancy and second in the ownership of cars and phones.

In 1929, its income per capita was 41 percent of that of the United States. The population suffered from mass unemployment and grinding poverty. In the 1950s, few Cuban children attended school and hardly any rural homes had electricity or running water. Almost 50 percent of rural Cubans could neither read nor write. Poverty and unemployment drove many Cubans from the countryside to Havana.

Cuba was a popular holiday destination due to its proximity to the USA. Wealthy Americans came to enjoy horse racing, gambling in its many casinos, and golf. President Fulgencio Batista had grand plans for more hotels and casinos before his downfall, with the prospect of Havana's waterfront being lined by them.

The economy was based on a single crop — sugar cane, and 90 percent of the country's raw sugar and tobacco exports was to the United States. Other national resources were in the hands of American companies such as the Bethlehem Steel Corporation and Speyer. US companies also owned Cuba's banks, the finance system, electric power production, and dominated Cuban industry. The best land on the island was owned by American monopolies, and profits from these investments went straight into the bank accounts of American businessmen.

Paseo de Marti o Prado

Marti or Prado Promenade

Prado Promenade, Havana, Cuba, 1920.

His next move was to try to change Cuban politics by restructuring the government. On February 24, 1961, four new ministries were created based on the Soviet model—Industries, Foreign Trade, Internal Trade, and Transport. Agriculture and Commerce were closed down. Che was appointed the first Minister of Industries in which role he had responsibility for the industrial operations of the Instituto Nacional de Reforma Agraria. It was a heady appointment, giving him virtually full control of the Cuban economy.

Che was at the height of his power, a staggering achievement for a man who just a few years previously had been little more than a hobo. He was now the revolution's main theoretician and a champion of global revolution. He had forged alliances with the socialist nations of the world and had stood up to American imperialism. He was a revolutionary statesman known around the world for his outspoken views and political achievements.

CATASTROPHE

Che delivered his policy for the Ministry of Industry on a radio show on May 3, 1961. He explained that industrialization would mean centralizing all industries. Factories working in the same sector of industry would be consolidated into *empresas consolidadas*, consolidated enterprises. He was still intent,

GUERRILLA WARFARE

• • • • • • • • • •

Che Guevara's manual for waging guerrilla warfare was written immediately after the Cuban Revolution and published in 1961 to acclaim by the Left and criticism by the Right. Although written to help other revolutionary movements around the world, it was also studied by the United States military so that they could learn how to combat guerrilla warfare. They took this learning to South American countries where they provided training for government troops.

In the book, Che gives three reasons for revolution—a lack of legitimacy by those governing the country; the existence of tensions that cannot be redressed by normal means; and the exhaustion of all legal efforts to bring change in a country. The book explains the "*foco* theory" (also known as focalism) which stipulates that small vanguards of fast-moving groups of combatants provide a focus for anger or discontent against an incumbent regime. This can lead to a general uprising.

Che claimed not to have read Mao Zedong's *On Guerrilla Warfare*, instead drawing on his own experiences in the Cuban Revolutionary War. He stressed that guerrilla methods required a political motivation, and should be employed only when trying to bring down a totalitarian regime where there is no other way to oppose it. The book was dedicated to his late rebel colleague Camilo Cienfuegos who, Che wrote, "should have read and corrected it, but whose fate prevented him from carrying out the task."

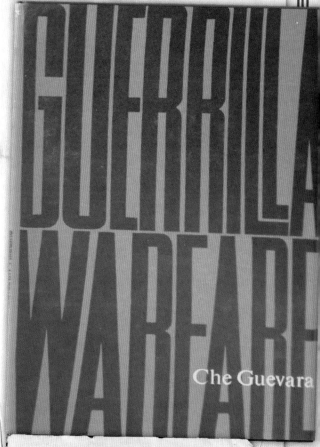

Book cover of *Guerrilla Warfare* published in 1961.

as he had been at the Banco Nacional, on diversification which meant a reduction in Cuba's dependency on sugar.

At that time, Che had disastrously cut back on sugar production and later confessed that it had been a catastrophe. He said:

> *Our first error was the way in which we carried out diversification. Instead of embarking on diversification by degrees, we attempted too much at once. The sugar cane areas were reduced and the land thus made available was used for cultivation of new crops. But this meant a general decline in agricultural production. The entire economic history of Cuba had demonstrated that no other agricultural activity would give such returns as those yielded by the cultivation of sugar cane. At the outset of the Revolution many of us were not aware of this basic economic fact, because a fetishistic idea connected sugar with our dependence on imperialism …*

It was an example of political philosophy getting in the way of sound economic sense and the low sugar harvests continued for several years. But the change from monoculture toward the production of a wider range of agricultural products was also too rapid and he admitted that:

> *Only a very solid productive organization could have resisted such a rapid change. In an underdeveloped country … the change … produced a greater weakness in the agricultural productive organization.*

FAILING FACTORIES

He could be proud of an increase in the production of electricity and the new industries that he created while in office. But in the industrial area he also made mistakes, caused he said by "a lack of precise understanding of the technological and economic elements necessary in the new industries installed during those years."

Factories had been put into operation in an effort to create jobs and end unemployment for many as well as to produce substitutes for the goods they were unable to import. Technically, however, these factories and their workers were inadequate. So, the second objective of substituting imported goods never really succeeded.

Indeed, productivity declined and workers stayed away from their places of work. Che believed fundamentally that the incentive to work should be the creation of a socialist state. Many of the benefits—paid holidays, for instance—workers had received under the old capitalist system had been withdrawn and the workers began to feel there was nothing to be gained from working. The situation was exacerbated by the fact that technicians and managers were badly trained.

Che enjoyed working alongside the ordinary citizens. It was his way of keeping fit and contributing to the community. In this photo by Osvaldo Salas he is seen during voluntary building work in Havana in 1961.

Alberto Korda captured this picture of a relaxed Che with his wife Aleida March walking through a crowded street in Havana, Cuba.

CHAPTER 10

THE BAY OF PIGS INVASION

Opposition to Castro's revolution did not just fade away however. Militant groups formed, planning to overthrow the regime, funded and supplied by various foreign entities, among whom were exiled Cubans in the United States, the CIA, and Rafael Trujillo's Dominican Republic.

On April 3, 1961, a bomb at the Army barracks at Bayamo killed four people, and three days later the Hershey Sugar factory at Matanzas was destroyed. On April 14, militant terrorists killed several revolutionary government troops near Las Cruces in Las Villas province.

Castro's retribution was swift, harsh, and decisive, throwing hundreds of counter-revolutionary opponents and US mercenaries into jail with long prison sentences. He also censored journalists and the press after articles began to appear criticizing the government's move toward the communist left.

CONSPIRING WITH THE MAFIA

Meanwhile, the United States government was increasingly critical of Castro's government and its single-party political system, suggesting that international communism was using Cuba as the hub for the spread of revolution in the West. Cuba's record on human rights and its removal of the freedom of the press were cited. But in this war of words, Castro gave as good as he got, referring to America's civil rights record and accusing the American media of being in the pocket of big business.

In August 1960 the CIA conspired with the Chicago Mafia to plan the simultaneous assassination of Fidel Castro, Raúl Castro, and Che Guevara. The quid pro quo if a new pro-US government was installed in Cuba, would be the Mafia reclaiming their former monopoly on gambling, prostitution, and drug dealing on the island.

Fidel Castro addresses an assembled crowd of Cuban militia civilian volunteers, April 1961.

OPERATION MONGOOSE

• • • • • • • • • •

General Edward Lansdale (1908 – 87) was given command of the "Cuban Project," also known as Operation Mongoose, a covert enterprise devised by the CIA but controlled by Attorney General Robert Kennedy (1925 – 68), brother of President Kennedy. The objective was to create an anti-Castro revolt in Cuba by October 1962. Based in Miami, Lansdale had a large budget of $50 million, four hundred CIA personnel, a small navy, and thousands of Cuban exiles who could be transported to Cuba to commit acts of sabotage, spread propaganda, and gather intelligence.

As many as thirty-three plans were devised, with options ranging from spreading anti-Castro propaganda and creating widespread disruption to plans that involved the use of US Army Special Forces, the mining of Cuban ports and harbors, and the destruction of the Cuban sugar crop precipitating economic catastrophe.

Efforts to assassinate Castro began as early as 1960. Many of the plans were outlandish, to say the least—pills containing poison, exploding seashells at his favorite diving locations and a toxin-lined diving suit, a ballpoint pen rigged up with a hypodermic needle, and the poisoning of his favorite cigars with botulinus toxin. One strange plan was to contaminate Castro's clothing with thallium salts so that his beard would fall out, making him look foolish in the eyes of his people.

A U-2 reconnaissance photo showing concrete evidence of missile assembly in Cuba.

ajor General Edward Lansdale.

SENATE { REPORT No. 94-755

FOREIGN AND MILITARY INTELLIGENCE

—

BOOK I

—

FINAL REPORT

OF THE

SELECT COMMITTEE

TC

First part of the Church Committee report on illegal intelligence gathering activities by US federal agencies.

THE BAY OF PIGS INVASION

In 1960 CIA Deputy Director Richard M. Bissell Jr. assembled a group of special agents to stage a counter-revolutionary military invasion of Cuba. Many of this experienced crew had already been involved in the CIA-backed 1954 Guatemala coup.

CIA agent Gerry Droller was tasked with recruiting a force of anti-Castro exiles in the Cuban-American community in the United States. Posing as wealthy steel tycoon "Frank Bender," Droller was assisted by CIA agent E. Howard Hunt calling himself "Eduardo." Hunt later gained notoriety as one of the "plumbers" involved in the Watergate break-in during the presidency of Richard M. Nixon.

Droller established training camps for the Cuban exiles in Florida and Guatemala, enlisting men and creating a force known as Brigade 2506. The area for the invasion was the Bay of Pigs on the southern coast of Cuba. It had an airfield nearby that could handle bombers, and was far removed from any civilians. There was not much military activity there, making future US denials of direct involvement more believable.

MOBILIZING THE MILITIA

Back in Florida, Cuban exiles formed the Cuban Revolutionary Council. Headed by former Prime Minister José Miró Cardona, it was effectively a government-in-waiting. Initially there were just twenty-eight men, commanded by José "Pepe" Peréz San Román but the numbers grew. Six B-26 bombers were obtained and ships were made ready to supply the operation.

Che suspected that there was going to be an invasion and for that reason he argued for the civilian population of Cuba to be armed into a fighting force:

> ... all of the Cuban people must become a guerrilla army; and each and every Cuban must learn to handle and if necessary use firearms in defense of the nation.

Che had seen what happened in Guatemala in 1954 and had no desire for a repeat performance in Cuba. He set about mobilizing a militia of the people. At the time Cuba had only 25,000 soldiers, with the police force numbering 9,000 and the navy 5,000. But Che organized the recruitment of a further 200,000 local militia volunteers.

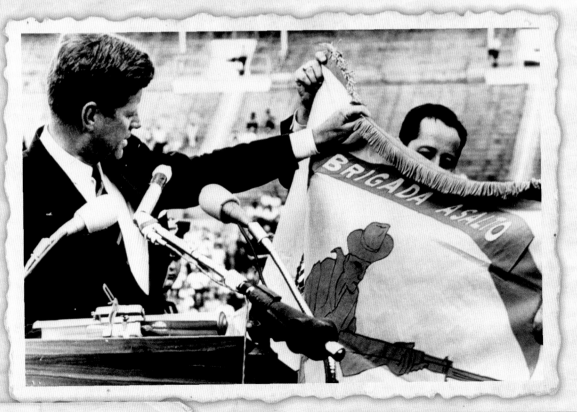

President Kennedy displays the combat flag of the Cuban assault brigade.

Cuban anti-aircraft gunners try to shoot down a US B-26 bomber during the Bay of Pigs invasion.

Most of these men were trained at the military schools that Che had established in the Sierra Maestra and at La Cabaña. Much of the credit for the success of the Cuban response to the invasion can be attributed to him, even though he personally played no part.

READY FOR THE FIGHT

On April 15, 1961, US planes from a CIA base in Nicaragua attacked the airports of Santiago de Cuba and San Antonio de los Baños. The Cuban Air Force base in Havana was also attacked. Seven people were killed and 53 were wounded. But this was merely the prelude to the invasion which took place after a raft of mock diversionary invasions.

On April 17, around 1,500 Cuban exiles landed at Playa Girón, a beach on the island's southern coast. Castro immediately left Havana at 2:30 a.m. and headed there to direct operations, trying to stop the invaders before they moved deeper into the island's interior. There was every chance that if they took a city, the situation could get out of hand. The exiles might proclaim an alternative government that

the US and other Latin American countries would immediately recognize as legitimate.

Leaked information about the attack had been filtering through to Cuba and by the time of the invasion, even its precise location was known. Castro had deployed his forces in that area in readiness. The rebels from the Sierra Maestra were on duty that night, familiar faces standing once again in the line of duty. Their experience in the Revolution stood them in good stead in the fierce battle that ensued. They were more than ready for the fight.

A DISASTER WAITING TO HAPPEN

President Kennedy was having second thoughts about the invasion, but the CIA assured him that local Cubans would be certain to fight alongside the invading exiles to rid the island of Castro. In the event this proved to be a false hope and even Cubans who were unhappy with Castro defended their country against what they saw as a foreign invasion.

The invading Cuban exiles themselves were expecting much more US help, but Kennedy had only reluctantly agreed to the invasion and had denied them the air support they so badly needed. Sixteen B-26 light attack bombers had been promised but this had been scaled back to eight by Kennedy. Not nearly enough to achieve their objectives. It was a disaster waiting to happen.

On the day of the invasion the Cuban Revolutionary Armed Forces were much better equipped and trained than anticipated. Only 135 of the invading force had actually been professionally trained as soldiers, and they soon found themselves pinned down, unable to advance inland or retreat, with only the sea behind them. The jungle terrain was impenetrable mangrove swamps, full of snakes and alligators, with swarms of mosquitoes and insects. They were trapped.

The following day, April 18, Kennedy authorized half a dozen jet fighters from the US aircraft carrier *Essex* to provide air cover for the B-26s. But incredibly the Pentagon got the time difference wrong between Cuba and Nicaragua, from where the B-26s took off, and the fighters missed their rendezvous by two hours.

FAILURE AND HUMILIATION

It was hopeless for the invaders and on the afternoon of April 19, just two days into their invasion, they surrendered. When Kennedy was informed of the mission's failure, he ordered two US destroyers to sail into the area to pick up survivors but they could only rescue those who had managed to swim out to one of the bay's numerous sandbars.

The beach was littered with bodies and Castro's men had taken prisoner 1,209 exiles of whom nine died en route to prison. The Cuban Army suffered 161 casualties. The prisoners were eventually exchanged by Castro for essential items such as baby food, powdered milk, medicines, and other goods to the value of around $60 million. It was a humiliation for the new US president.

An American plane shot down on Playa Girón by Cuban anti-aircraft batteries.

Defensive artillery fires against the invading CIA-backed Cuban exiles as they come ashore at the Bay of Pigs.

A BRUSH WITH DEATH

Meanwhile, Che was wounded in a careless accident. He was commanding a force in Pinar del Río, the stretch of Cuban coastline closest to the United States, Castro having been concerned that a second attack might quickly follow. He accidentally dropped his revolver with the safety catch switched off.

This was strictly against regulations and if he had caught one of his men doing this, he would certainly have punished him. The gun went off and the bullet entered his cheek and emerged just below his ear. He was a very lucky man. It certainly was a close brush with death.

A STEEP LEARNING CURVE

Castro tried to further embarrass Kennedy with speeches accusing him of picking on his smaller and less well-off neighbors. This only served to increase Kennedy's desire to remove the Cuban from power. It was a strange face-off because Cuba could hardly be considered a threat to the huge and very powerful nation to the north. "A thorn in the flesh, not a dagger at the heart," as Senator J. William Fulbright described it.

The Bay of Pigs invasion was part of a steep learning curve for Kennedy early in his presidency. He had hoped to make an impact on the Soviet Union as a president who meant business, but the invasion fiasco made Kennedy look vulnerable to Russian leader Nikita Khrushchev. Perhaps Khrushchev took this weakness into account when he decided to install nuclear missiles on Cuban soil. Fortunately, Kennedy had learned a lot by this time and handled the missile crisis adroitly.

Some have speculated over the years that Kennedy's assassination was somehow connected to Cuba. One Kennedy aide wrote that by 1963 Kennedy's administration had begun secret talks with the Cubans that both sides hoped might lead to peaceful coexistence. This approach angered the Cuban exiles whose main objective was to remove Castro from office. They are said by some to have been behind President Kennedy's assassination. But this, of course, is just one of countless conspiracy theories about the president's murder.

There is also a belief that the USA's and the CIA's antipathy to Castro may even have helped prolong his years in office. Cubans do not take kindly to foreign intervention and preferred to have Castro in power rather than a US puppet.

LEADING BY EXAMPLE

Che in the meantime was getting on with the business of government. He traveled relentlessly across the island, visiting factories, and delivering uplifting speeches. He often arrived completely unannounced asking to see the attendance register to check absenteeism, aware that Cubans were not famous for working long hours or even working at all. He was always welcomed by cheering crowds wherever he went. His charismatic personality shone through his words about five-year plans and production schedules.

His speeches were filled with lengthy exhortations to produce more and work harder. They should go to work no matter what, he said, and not to use militia patrol duty or political training as an excuse to avoid work.

He told them that he himself worked every hour of the day and most of the night and on Sunday joined a volunteer work party to cut sugar cane. He even took his wife along despite the pressures that she faced, working in his office all week and bringing up a family.

He was leading by example, and delivered all these speeches with a smile on his face, mainly because he was genuinely enjoying himself so much.

THE ALLIANCE FOR PROGRESS

The Inter-American Economic and Social Council of the Organization of American States (OAS) was meeting in August 1961 at the seaside resort of Punta del Este, Uruguay, and Che took a large Cuban delegation there. The conference was launching an initiative dreamed up by President Kennedy—the Alliance for Progress.

The Cuban delegation was based at the Hotel Playa and the American delegation, led by Treasury Secretary C. Douglas Dillon, was billeted at the Vanguard. The atmosphere was tense and people waited expectantly to watch sparks fly between Che and the Americans.

Kennedy's plan was presented, but Che saw through it immediately. More aid from

During a speech at the Inter-American Economic and Social Conference, Che accused the United States of plotting to assassinate Fidel Castro and provoke armed aggression.

the USA would allow the other countries in Central and South America to buy imported goods instead of establishing their own export industries.

Che spoke on August 8, denouncing the Alliance for Progress and accusing the American president of trying to maintain US control over the Americas, dressing it up differently, but presenting the same old ideas. A nation must be free, he said, and quoted José Martí from many decades previously:

> Whoever speaks of economic union speaks of political union. The nation that buys, commands; the nation that sells, serves. Commerce must be balanced to assure freedom. A nation that wants to die sells to one nation only, and a nation that would be saved sells to more than one. The excessive influence of one country over another's commerce becomes political influence … A nation that wants to be free must be free in matters of trade.

RIPPING INTO THE USA

It was also a golden opportunity to rip into the USA. Che began by berating all their attacks on Cuba—the burning of sugar cane fields, the refusal of US oil companies to refine Russian oil, the sabotage of the steamship *La Coubre* at Havana's docks, and the invasion at the Bay of Pigs.

He went on to demand the independence of all occupied territories—the Panama Canal Zone, the Malvinas Islands (the Falklands), Swan Island off the coast of Honduras, the Guianas in north-eastern South America, and the British Antilles in the Caribbean.

He trumpeted Cuba's achievements, paying tribute to their progressive civil freedoms whereby women and all races, regardless of color, had been given equal rights. He celebrated the Cuban government's success in virtually eliminating illiteracy. He finished off by rebuking the USA for not helping the other nations of America to develop their own industries.

MEETING KENNEDY'S ENVOY

The press were fascinated by the glamorous politician in army fatigues, and he was followed everywhere by photographers and cameramen like a film star, which he found rather amusing. But he also had a chance to meet up with family and friends who had crossed the River Plate to Uruguay from Buenos Aires, and he spent time with them between speeches and engagements.

One of those engagements was a meeting with Richard N. Goodwin, a personal envoy of President Kennedy. The opportunity arose during a birthday party held for a Brazilian diplomat. Che began by requesting that Goodwin thank Kennedy for the Bay of Pigs invasion. The incident and Cuba's subsequent success had helped consolidate the Revolution at a critical time.

He told Goodwin that Kennedy had handed the Revolution over to "us," by which he meant the Marxists in the Cuban government. He did offer something of an olive branch, however, seeking a means by which the two countries could coexist and even offering compensation for the seizure of American businesses that had taken place.

He said Cuba could agree that she would not ally with the countries of the socialist bloc but he could not apologize for the natural affinity that Cuba had for them. Perhaps elections could even be allowed in Cuba once the Revolution was assured.

Finally, he complained about the US base on Cuba at Guantánamo, insisting that it was a violation of Cuban sovereignty. He ended by saying that the United States would have to cease its covert operations in Latin America and stop trying to topple the government of Cuba. He told Goodwin that he would only speak of their meeting to Castro and in return Goodwin promised his complete discretion.

JOHN F. KENNEDY

John Fitzgerald Kennedy was born in 1917 in Brookline, Massachusetts, his father and mother scions of two wealthy Irish-Catholic Boston families. His father Joseph (1888 – 1969) was a banker who made a fortune on the stock market after World War I, and was US Ambassador to the United Kingdom from 1938 to 1940. Nicknamed Jack, John Kennedy was the second oldest of nine siblings for whom their father had huge expectations.

The young Jack was not a good student but managed to get into the elite Connecticut prep school Choate, and then into Princeton, where he spent one semester before enrolling at Harvard in 1936. He was a sickly child and adolescent, suffering from debilitating colds, scarlet fever, and undiagnosed stomach ailments that forced him to miss large chunks of his education.

When the United States entered World War II, Kennedy enlisted in the US Navy, and was given command of a patrol torpedo boat in the South Pacific. In August 1943, his vessel was rammed by a Japanese warship. Two of his crew lost their lives and Kennedy led the surviving members to a nearby island where they were rescued six days later. The incident captured headlines and earned him the Navy and Marine Corps Medal and a Purple Heart.

Thanks to his father's money and his status as a war hero, he won a seat in the US House of Representatives as a Democrat. He served from 1946 to 1952, and then ran for the Senate. He was Senator for Massachusetts from 1953 to 1960. He won the Democratic presidential nomination in 1960. After a scintillating campaign, he defeated Richard Nixon to become the 35th President of the United States. At 43, he was the second youngest president in history.

Kennedy's presidency was marked by a number of dangerous crises. The Bay of Pigs was a

disaster but he was given credit for his handling of the Cuban Missile Crisis. In domestic affairs, civil rights changes he proposed were blocked by southern Democrats. His Civil Rights Bill was finally passed by Congress in 1964, after his death.

President Kennedy was assassinated by Lee Harvey Oswald in Dallas on November 22, 1963. He was 46 years old and had been in office for 1,036 days. To the American people he remains a hero who created a White House that became known as "Camelot." He persistently rates among the most beloved of US presidents, alongside Abraham Lincoln and Thomas Jefferson.

NIKITA KHRUSHCHEV

Nikita Sergeyevich Khrushchev (1894 – 1971) was born into a poor family in the village of Kalinovka, in south-west Russia. When he was 14, he became an apprentice metal-fitter, and later worked in a mine in Rutchenkovo.

In 1917, after the abdication of Tsar Nicholas II, Khrushchev was elected to the Rutchenkovo worker's council, or soviet, and soon became chairman. He joined the Bolshevik Party in 1918 and served in the Red Army during the Russian Civil War. In 1921, he was assigned as assistant director for political affairs to the Rutchenkovo mine. In mid-1925 he attended the 14th Congress of the USSR Communist party in Moscow.

He began to rise through the party ranks and became a close associate of Stalin, playing a part in the Great Purge in which millions of Russians were executed or sent to the Gulag labor camps. He returned to the Ukraine in 1937 as head of the Communist Party there, and following his arrival the pace of the purge accelerated.

During World War II, Khrushchev served on many fronts, used by Stalin to keep his commanders under tight control. On returning to Ukraine in 1943, he found it devastated by the occupying Germans. He began the work of rebuilding the region. In 1949, he was recalled to Moscow, serving as head of the Moscow Party.

Following Stalin's death in 1953, Khrushchev became leader of the Soviet Union but took several years to consolidate his position. In 1956, at the 20th Party Congress, he delivered the "Secret Speech," revealing Stalin's crimes for the first time, and began a process called "de-Stalinization." He improved living standards, traveled to the West, and invested in the space program, but always kept a tight grip on power in the Kremlin.

But in 1962, facing Kennedy, he backed down over the Cuban Missile Crisis. Party officials were dismayed and, along with some years of poor economic growth and poor relations with China, his enemies had the opportunity to depose him.

Khrushchev served as Soviet Premier until October 14, 1964, but was retired by the party due to his advanced age and poor health. He was given an apartment in Moscow and a villa in the countryside. He died seven years later of heart disease, at the age of 77, on September 11, 1971.

CHAPTER 11

THE CUBAN MISSILE CRISIS

On August 19, 1961, Che boarded a small aircraft at dawn, and flew to the tiny Don Torcuato airstrip eighteen miles from Buenos Aires. The trip was a secret visit to the Argentine President Arturo Frondizi (1908 – 95) who saw himself as a peacemaker between the United States and Cuban governments. Frondizi hoped to prevent trouble breaking out between the two nations which would be bad for the entire continent, but he also wanted to build a reputation for himself as an international statesman.

Frondizi had been constantly under threat of a military coup by the army, and if he could find a way to make himself indispensable it would delay the inevitable overthrow by the generals. The presidential aides sent to the airfield were astonished when they saw Che walk down the aircraft steps.

The generals would not be amused if they were to find out the Cuban front man was visiting behind their backs. The aides quietly drove Che to the Argentinean presidential residence in Buenos Aires, careful to keep their precious cargo undercover.

REVOLUTION IS THE ONLY OPTION

When Che arrived, he explained to Frondizi that Cuba wanted to come to an agreement with the Americans so that the two countries could coexist peacefully. He made it clear that Cuba had no desire to be tied too closely to the USSR, despite the aid the Cubans were receiving from the Russians. Cuba wished to be an autonomous socialist state but sometimes, Che said, violent revolution was the only option for small, poor nations.

Frondizi did not concur. Che was wrong, the president said, and asked if he had read Marx to which the revolutionary replied that he had not, perhaps somewhat disingenuously. But he did admit to the president that the opponents of the Revolution who had been shot by firing squad had become heroes for some, and that the redistribution of land had not always brought the desired results. Che welcomed the possibility of Argentina mediating between Cuba and the United States.

Arturo Frondizi, President of Argentina from 1958 to 1962.

As this fairly cordial meeting drew to a close, Che asked Frondizi for a favor. He asked if he could be driven to the home of his aunt, María Luisa Guevara-Lynch de Martínez-Castro, a sister of his father, who was very ill and likely to die. Frondizi was reluctant because of the dangers inherent in an unplanned journey, but finally agreed. Che managed to spend a few minutes with his aunt before leaving for the airfield and his flight back to Montevideo.

As predicted, the military generals were furious when they discovered that Che had secretly been in Argentina, and Frondizi did not last long as president after that. He was quickly deposed and exiled to the island of Martín García.

A SHINING LIGHT

December 1961 brought to a close an extraordinary year-long literacy campaign. Castro had delivered a speech at the United Nations in New York the previous year in which he promised to end illiteracy in Cuba.

During the year that followed, uniformed students traveled the length and breadth of the island delivering a literacy program to countless Cubans who had never been taught how to read and write.

Sadly, forty of these student volunteers lost their lives in the process, killed by opponents of the Revolution who still hid in the mountains. But it was a shining light for the rest of the American continent which had never seen such a campaign.

BAD ADVICE

Richard Goodwin returned to Washington after his meeting with Che at the Alliance for Progress conference in Uruguay. He brought Kennedy a box of Cuban cigars, a gift for the president from Castro. Amusingly, Kennedy is said to have asked Goodwin to light his first just in case Castro had sent him exploding cigars, a tactic considered by the CIA to eliminate the Cuban leader. Later Goodwin wrote a memo to Kennedy outlining what he and Che had discussed. It would not have made good reading for Che, had he seen it.

US Strategic Air Command personnel interpreting reconnaissance photographs.

Goodwin recommended to Kennedy that the blockade on Cuba should be increased, and the country should be excluded from international conferences and meetings like the one he and Che had just attended. He told Kennedy to pay no attention to Castro's pleas for peaceful coexistence and said that the work of weakening the regime by promulgating anti-Castro propaganda should continue and be intensified.

He believed that the USSR would not provide financial aid to Cuba, and suggested that Che was speaking from a position of weakness. After the meeting with Goodwin, Kennedy immediately reinstated Operation Mongoose. Regrettably Goodwin had totally misjudged the situation, and once more Kennedy's aides were advising him badly and feeding him unreliable information.

On January 21, 1962, the Organization of American States (OAS) held the Eighth Meeting of Consultation of the Ministers of Foreign Affairs in Punta del Este, Uruguay. The United States encouraged Central American representatives to advocate a hard-line against Castro, and support sanctions against Cuba. Despite being a founding member of the OAS, Cuba was effectively suspended from January 31, 1962.

SECOND DECLARATION OF HAVANA

In Cuba, as a response to its expulsion from the OAS, on February 4, 1962, Castro issued the Second Declaration of Havana, described by some as one of the greatest historical documents of all time. Delivering it to the People's General Assembly in Plaza de la Revolución José Martí, Castro denounced the Americans and the Bay of Pigs invasion, reaffirming his determination to resist American plans to bring down his government.

He delivered an historical analysis of the revolutionary and political situation in Latin America and the exploitation by imperialists that he claimed it had engendered. Castro's speeches were never short and this one was

no exception, but one part resonated with his massive audience:

We will resist on every single battle site: we will resist on the economic battleground, we will persist in advancing on the cultural front … Our Fatherland is not toiling away for today. Rather, our Fatherland sweats for tomorrow. And this will be a tomorrow, overflowing with promises that nobody will be able to snatch away from us; no one will be able to deny us it, because with our people's pietas, we are going to win it; through our people's bravery and heroism, we are going to conquer.

ENOUGH IS ENOUGH

Castro declared that if America or anyone else attacked Cuba the poor would rise up in a wave of "fibrillating rancor, justice demanded and rights that had been trampled. A wave that is beginning to surge throughout the lands of Latin America." Castro ended with Che's rallying call at the United Nations:

Because this great humanity has said "enough's enough!" and has awoken. Because this march of giants will not stop until it has won true independence; because they have died more than once in vain. Today, in any event, those that may die, will die like those in Cuba, those at the Bay of Pigs. They will die for a single, genuine independence that can never be given up.

Che was present when Castro delivered his speech, as were many of the rebels. He made it clear that for countries denied industrialization around the world and exploited by the great powers, there was only one option—revolution. His words provided inspiration and impetus to guerrilla movements all across Latin America.

Che's theory of the armed struggle being the way to freedom for suppressed countries was gaining momentum. The Second Declaration of Havana showed that Cuba wanted to export revolution to other Latin American countries. As the key architect and political theorist of the Cuban Revolution, it was mainly Che's work.

BEGINNING OF A BITTER FEELING

For the Soviets it was a disappointment, to all intents and purposes, Cuba was following the Maoist line. But if they did not want to drive the revolutionaries into Chinese hands, they had to accept it. It was the beginning of a bitter feeling between Che and Moscow.

Indeed, Cuba was now providing funding and training for many other guerrilla movements. Che's *Guerrilla Warfare* served as their manual. The Russians helped too, after the Cuban Minister of Internal Affairs, Ramiro Valdés, made efforts to bring the Russians onboard to help in the training of revolutionaries. He used their ongoing rivalry with China to encourage them, claiming that the Russians were lagging behind the Chinese in influence around the world.

Soviet premier Khrushchev listened and increased aid in the form of armaments and personnel which indirectly helped in the training of the revolutionaries who came to Cuba from all over Latin America.

RATION BOOK EQUALITY

In March 1962, ration books were issued in Cuba. Castro spoke on television about the need for such a move, describing it as a way to distribute food and other products fairly to the people. In fact, the ration book is still used today. When Che heard people complain that the ration was not enough to live on, he retorted that his family seemed to get by okay.

Then someone pointed out that he had two ration books, one for being a government minister and another book for his rank of comandante. Che rushed home to check this and, finding it to be true, immediately told Aleida to return one of them. He wanted to live on the same ration as everyone else.

The following month, he chaired the closing session of the National Council of the Center de Trabajadores de Cuba. He said in his address that:

> *The Revolution has to be carried out at a violent pace; anyone who tires has the right to tire but not the right to call themselves part of the vanguard.*

Che with Nikita Khrushchev in Moscow, 1962.

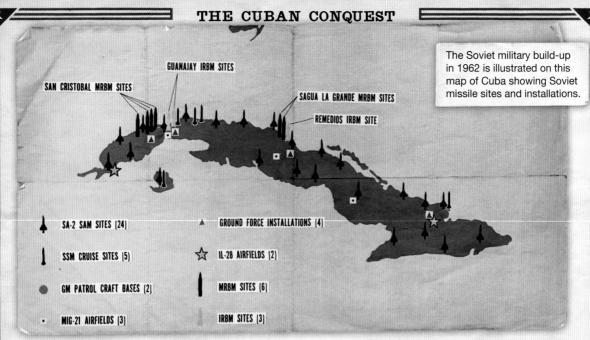

GUANAJAY IRBM SITES

SAN CRISTOBAL MRBM SITES

SAGUA LA GRANDE MRBM SITES

REMEDIOS IRBM SITE

The Soviet military build-up in 1962 is illustrated on this map of Cuba showing Soviet missile sites and installations.

SA-2 SAM SITES (24)

SSM CRUISE SITES (5)

GM PATROL CRAFT BASES (2)

MIG-21 AIRFIELDS (3)

GROUND FORCE INSTALLATIONS (4)

IL-28 AIRFIELDS (2)

MRBM SITES (6)

IRBM SITES (3)

In May, Aleida gave birth to his son Camilo, named after his late rebel friend Camilo Cienfuegos. Che was delighted to have a son and heir.

SENDING SOVIET MISSILES TO CUBA

Toward the end of August 1962, there was more government business when Che and Emilio Aragonés flew to Moscow for talks about cooperation on a whole raft of issues including agriculture, steel, and technology. They signed agreements in Yalta at the beginning of September and were back in Havana on September 6.

It was a significant trip during which Che and Aragonés met with Khrushchev on August 30 at his summer house in the Crimea. The Russian leader had in July already made a secret agreement with Fidel Castro and his brother to install Soviet ballistic missiles on Cuban soil as a response and deterrent against another US invasion like the Bay of Pigs.

Che and Aragonés expressed their concern about the reaction of the United States to such a move. But Khrushchev was adamant that the missiles be installed, insisting that he would send the Baltic fleet to the region if the Americans objected.

EXPERT EYES

The United States had been sending U-2 surveillance missions over Cuba since the Bay of Pigs fiasco. But it was not until October 14 that the first unsettling photographic images were obtained by a U-2 spy plane piloted by Major Richard Heyser.

Outwardly, the images just showed a field near San Cristobál in Pinar del Río, and when Robert Kennedy was shown the image by his brother the president on October 16, he reckoned it looked like a football pitch. But expert eyes at the Pentagon had analyzed the U-2 imagery in great detail and knew only too well what they were seeing—a ballistic missile site under construction.

There were areas set aside for missile launchers, stations for missile trailers, and tented sections for personnel. The CIA worked out from around a thousand U-2 photographs that the missiles were similar to those with nuclear capabilities seen at the Soviet military parades in Red Square, Moscow. Estimates that the missiles could be operational in about a week were even more concerning.

Other nearby installations were also spotted by the U-2s, suitable for between sixteen and thirty-two missiles. The nuclear missiles had a range of around 1,600 miles. Well within the distance of many American cities, they had the potential to kill as many as 80 million Americans.

RAMPING UP THE CRISIS

When President Kennedy appeared on television on October 22, criticizing the Soviet Union's actions in Cuba and declaring a naval blockade of the island, the crisis ramped up another notch. He had also warned the Pentagon to be ready for military action, explaining:

It shall be the policy of this nation to regard any nuclear missile launched from Cuba against any nation in the Western Hemisphere as an attack by the Soviet Union on the United States, requiring a full retaliatory response upon the Soviet Union … To halt this offensive build-up, a strict quarantine on all offensive military equipment under shipment to Cuba is being initiated. All ships of any kind bound for Cuba, from whatever nation or port, will, if found to contain cargoes of offensive weapons, be turned back. This quarantine will be extended, if needed, to other types of cargo and carriers. We are not at this time, however, denying the necessities of life as the Soviets attempted to do in their Berlin blockade of 1948.

The following day, Khrushchev denounced the American blockade. He said the missiles were designed to prevent war, not start it. He also believed that Kennedy had been bluffing in his television address, just to look tough and decisive to the American people in the wake of the Bay of Pigs fiasco.

THE DANGEROUS GAME

Jousting between the two world leaders had started almost as soon as Kennedy had moved into the White House. At the Vienna summit conference in June 1961, they had clashed over the fate of West Berlin. Kennedy had been satisfied with what he thought he had achieved in Vienna, but just two months later, East Germany suddenly closed its border with West Berlin and began building the Berlin Wall. The two halves of the city remained divided for almost three decades.

Ballistic missiles in Cuba were just another part of the dangerous game of confrontation that America and the Soviet Union were playing. America had similar missiles in Italy and Turkey that had the capability of taking out most Russian cities.

Russian students demonstrating against the US blockade of Cuba.

The Soviet premier felt that Russia was merely keeping up by basing missiles with nuclear warheads in Cuba. Anyway, America had almost 3,000 nuclear warheads and 300 missile launchers; many more than the Russians who had just 250 warheads including those being installed in Cuba.

Castro had initially been against the installation of the missiles but eventually came round to the idea:

> We did not like the missiles. If it was a matter of our defense alone, we would not have accepted the missiles here. But do not think it was because of the dangers that would come from having the missiles here, but rather because of the way this could damage the image of the Revolution in Latin America.

90 MILES FROM FLORIDA

Between June and October 1962, the number of Soviet personnel in Cuba preparing for the installation reached as many as 42,000. Dozens of ships crossed the ocean to Cuba in that time. It is astonishing that America only noticed all this activity at the last moment. By the first few days of October, thirty-six R-12 medium-range missiles had already been installed and the White House had to deny charges that it was ignoring dangerous Soviet missiles just 90 miles (140 km) from Florida.

Following Kennedy's declaration of a naval blockade on October 22, Cuba mobilized its population, and the Cuban militia were put on stand-by again. Castro was convinced that the Americans were about to launch another invasion and deployed his forces accordingly, sending Che to command the troops based at Pinar del Río. Once there Che established his headquarters in a mountain cave that was close to the missile site at San Cristóbal but it had to be damp-proofed first because of his asthma.

On October 24, Castro denounced Kennedy as the world worried just how far this was going to go. Meanwhile, fourteen ships that were carrying cargo from the USSR to Cuba were instructed to turn away from the area that American ships were blockading. Nonetheless, there was no slow-down in the installation of the missiles.

On October 26, Kennedy told his National Security Committee (EXCOMM) that he believed the only way that the missiles could be removed was to invade Cuba. He was persuaded, however, to hold back and continue with diplomatic and military pressure. The number of low-level flights over the island were doubled and plans were rapidly put together to establish a new government in Cuba if ultimately America did have to invade.

THE DIPLOMATIC DEAL

On October 26, John A. Scali, political correspondent for ABC News, was asked to lunch by Aleksandr Fomin, the undercover name of the KGB station chief in Washington. Scali had already eaten lunch when Fomin called him, but the Russian's voice was so urgent and insistent that Scali decided to drop everything and go immediately. The two men met at the old Occidental Restaurant, two blocks from the White House.

The KGB agent asked Scali to speak to his high-level contacts in Washington to find out if the United States would possibly entertain a diplomatic solution to the missile crisis. In the days that followed, John Scali became a pivotal go-between, courier, and spokesman for the US government as an urgent resolution was negotiated.

Eventually Aleksandr Fomin put an offer on the table that was hard to refuse. Russia could agree for the missiles to be removed under United Nations supervision, and Castro would assure the world that he would not accept such weapons on Cuban soil again, if in return the United States gave a public undertaking not to invade Cuba.

America jumped at the opportunity of such a diplomatic deal, and a message was conveyed to Castro via the Scali-Fomin connection that America would be "unlikely to invade," if the missiles were removed from the island.

THE ARMAGEDDON LETTER

Around 6:00 p.m. on October 26, a long letter started to come in, written personally by the Soviet premier. It has been described as a "long and emotional" missive and in it Khrushchev reiterated what had been suggested to Scali earlier that day:

> I propose: we, for our part, will declare that our ships bound for Cuba are not carrying any armaments. You will declare that the United States will not invade Cuba with its troops and will not support any other forces which might intend to invade Cuba. Then the necessity of the presence of our military specialists in Cuba will disappear.

Still convinced that an invasion by US troops was imminent, Castro ordered his anti-aircraft guns to shoot down any US aircraft on sight over Cuban territory. He also sent a message to Khrushchev demanding a pre-emptive nuclear missile strike on the USA. The letter received the following day is now known as the "Armageddon Letter," in which Castro wrote:

> I believe the imperialists' aggressiveness is extremely dangerous and if they actually carry out the brutal act of invading Cuba in violation of international law and morality, that would be the moment to eliminate such danger forever through an act of clear legitimate defense, however harsh and terrible the solution would be.

THE JUPITER MISSILES IN EUROPE

At dawn on October 27, the CIA informed Kennedy that a number of the Soviet missile sites now appeared to be fully operational and Cuban forces were ready for action. But later that morning Moscow radio broadcast a message from Khrushchev that was different to the one he had transmitted the previous evening.

In return for removing Soviet missiles from Cuba, he now wanted the removal of the US Jupiter ballistic missiles in Turkey and Italy. It seemed obvious to US officials that Khrushchev had come under pressure from party officials in the Kremlin. A message followed a few hours later, the Soviet premier making his new demand official:

> You are disturbed over Cuba. You say that this disturbs you because it is ninety-nine miles by sea from the coast of the United States of America. But ... you have placed destructive missile weapons, which you call offensive, in Italy and Turkey, literally next to us ... I therefore make this proposal: We are willing to remove from Cuba the means which you regard as offensive ... Your representatives will make a declaration to the effect that the United States ... will remove its analogous means from Turkey ... and after that, persons entrusted by the United Nations Security Council could inspect on the spot the fulfilment of the pledges made.

The Soviets did not know that the Americans were planning to remove the Jupiter missiles from Turkey anyway. They were obsolete and being replaced by Polaris nuclear ballistic missiles carried by submarines.

TENSION RISING

On the morning of October 27, a trespassing American U-2 was shot down over Cuba and the pilot was killed. Tension was rising. It had been agreed that if a spy plane was shot down it would represent an intentional escalation of hostilities and America would attack Cuba, but in the event there was no US retaliation, and the stand-off continued.

That evening, it was decided to revert to Khrushchev's original deal. The letter containing this offer was accompanied by an oral message to the effect that a failure to remove the missiles would result in military action by the United States. The message did not mention Turkey but there would be an understanding that those missiles would be removed "voluntarily."

It was fully expected that war could break out as early as the following day. The USA finalized plans for air strikes on the missile sites and other strategic targets such as petrol storage facilities. Washington warned America's European allies shortly after midnight that:

> *The situation is growing shorter ... the United States may find it necessary within a very short time in its interest and that of its fellow nations in the Western Hemisphere to take whatever military action may be necessary.*

BLACK SATURDAY

The next day was dubbed "Black Saturday" by the White House. It was a war of nerves as America and Russia tested each other's patience.

US practice depth charges about the size of hand grenades were dropped on a Soviet submarine which came too close to the border of the blockade line. What the US Navy did not know was that the submarine was armed with a nuclear torpedo and they were under orders to fire should its hull be breached in an attack. Agreement from all three officers on board was necessary to launch the torpedo but one of them, Vasili Arkhipov, voted against the launch and so prevented a Soviet nuclear strike.

The debris of an American U-2 piloted by Rudolph Anderson and shot down over Cuba during the 1962 missile crisis.

That same Black Saturday, a U-2 spy plane mistakenly flew into Soviet air space for ninety minutes which resulted in Soviet MiG fighters taking off from Wrangel Island while the Americans scrambled F-102 fighters over the Bering Sea armed with nuclear air-to-air missiles.

THE MISSILE SWAP

On October 27 after more talks, Kennedy gave Khrushchev a secret reassurance that he would quietly remove all the missiles in southern Italy and Turkey in exchange for the removal of the Cuban missiles. At 9:00 a.m. on the morning of October 28, Khrushchev's latest message was broadcast on Russian radio.

Khrushchev stated that the Soviet government had ordered the dismantling of the missiles and their return to the USSR. Kennedy reckoned it would appear to be a pretty even swap, America's Turkish missiles for Russia's Cuban ones. Kennedy wrote back to Khrushchev:

I consider my letter to you of October twenty-seventh and your reply of today as firm undertakings on the part of both our governments which should be promptly carried out … The US will make a statement in the framework of the Security Council in reference to Cuba as follows: it will declare that the United States of America will respect the inviolability of Cuban borders, its sovereignty, that it take the pledge not to interfere in internal affairs, not to intrude themselves and not to permit our territory to be used as a bridgehead for the invasion of Cuba, and will restrain those who would plan to carry an aggression against Cuba, either from US territory or from the territory of other countries neighboring to Cuba.

In the next few days, it became evident that the Soviets were indeed dismantling the missile sites and shipping everything back to Russia.

BACK FROM THE BRINK

Ultimately, it was never made public that the US missiles were being removed from Italy and Turkey, and it appeared to the American people that Khrushchev had lost face and been somewhat humiliated. But one theory has it that the cunning Russian leader had only cleverly agreed with Castro to install the missiles in Cuba as a bargaining chip in his efforts to have the US missiles removed.

Whatever the reason, the end-result was that the United States had given a very public undertaking that it would not invade Cuba. It had been thirteen days of aggressive confrontation and war-mongering, but finally the world had been pulled back from the very brink of a nuclear holocaust.

FEELINGS OF BETRAYAL

Cuba felt betrayed by the Soviet Union and Castro disappeared to his home in the Sierra Maestra for time to reflect. Decisions had all along been made in Washington and Moscow with very little reference to Havana. Castro was disappointed that certain matters had not been resolved in the negotiations such as the US base at Guantánamo Bay on Cuba. Relations between the two countries were poor for a number of the following years, but Cuba could ill-afford to completely cut off contact with the Soviets.

When all the offensive missiles and Russian bombers had been withdrawn from Cuba, the US naval blockade was formally ended on November 21, 1962. The last US missiles in Turkey were not finally dismantled until late April 1963.

The CIA's Operation Mongoose was officially wound down toward the end of 1962, but US undercover sabotage of Cuba's government, shipping, and installations continued. Under the auspices of President Kennedy, the covert actions were carried out by the ever-willing Cuban exiles, forever keen to hit back at the revolutionaries in as many ways as humanly possible.

CHAPTER 12

THE PRICE OF GLORY

In an interview with a journalist from the British communist newspaper, *The Daily Worker*, Che said that if the missiles had been operated by Cubans they would undoubtedly have been launched. "If someone is out to get you," he added, "you have no choice but to fight to the death." He very obviously still perceived violence to be the only way to achieve revolution. Like Castro, he was also very disillusioned with the behavior of the Soviet Union.

A VISIT FROM CELIA

Che's mother, Celia, was a political activist and had become an excellent public speaker. In October 1962, on her way to Europe to see the sights, she dropped in on her son and her grandchildren in Havana. She had flown from Buenos Aires to Montevideo where she had spoken at a pro-Cuban rally. She experienced the missile crisis in Cuba, seeing the danger that her son faced on a daily basis during that time.

She had recovered from breast cancer but it had recurred and she was not in the best of health. Nonetheless, she was delighted to visit her son and accompanied Che on a few of his trips around his adopted country. It must have thrilled her to see how her son was welcomed wherever he went and the obvious love that the Cuban people had for him.

He explained to her his scheme of getting people to volunteer to cut cane sugar, as he did most Sundays when he could. He told her that it relaxed him, that he could leave all his problems behind and, of course, it provided him with much-needed exercise.

A CULTURAL REVOLUTION

A program promoting Cuban culture was launched with new museums, art schools, and theaters being opened. Cervantes' *Don Quixote de la Mancha* was distributed free to the people, and musicians were guaranteed a wage. Many foreign artists and performers visited the island. The brain behind it all was journalist

Che and his mother Celia de la Serna in 1962.

CARLOS FRANQUI

Carlos Franqui (1921 – 2010) joined the Communist Party of Cuba, and at age 20 he became an organizer for the party, working to build membership in small towns. He turned to journalism to earn his living and became involved in several literary and artistic movements.

His association with Fidel Castro's 26th of July Movement began in 1952, when Franqui became editor of the underground newspaper *Revolución*, working in secret in Havana. He was the first journalist to print that Castro had landed on the Cuban coast and was in the Sierra Maestra with his fellow rebels and for this he was arrested, imprisoned, and tortured. Released from prison he went into exile, firstly in Mexico and then in Florida. Soon, Castro called for his return to Cuba and he worked again on *Revolución* in the mountains as well as on the rebels' radio station, Radio Rebelde.

Revolución became the official organ of the Cuban government with Franqui as editor of the newspaper. He focused on literature and the arts and met world-famous artists and intellectuals, several of whom traveled to Cuba to see the revolution first-hand. But, he did not always see eye to eye with the state authorities. Eventually he was forced to resign, and *Revolución* was shut down.

He turned his attention to running art projects, but his disagreements with the government persisted. After many disputes, he was allowed to leave the island, settling in Italy where he promoted Cuban art and culture although he received no payment for his work.

When the USSR invaded Czechoslovakia in 1968, Franqui was a signatory to a letter condemning the act, leading to a complete break with the Cuban government. Franqui wrote several books telling the story of the revolution, and campaigned against repression in Castro's Cuba. He was officially named a traitor by Cuba and accused of being a CIA spy.

Semi-retired in the 1990s, he relocated to Puerto Rico where he founded *Carta de Cuba*, publishing work by Cuban writers. He died in Puerto Rico in 2010, at age 88.

Carlos Franqui (center) with French intellectuals Jean-Paul Sartre (left) and Simone de Beauvoir (second left) in Havana, 1960.

Carlos Franqui. The aim was to hit back at the wave of US culture that was beginning to engulf the world in music, film, and television, and to create a specific Afro-Cuban culture.

The state, however, liked to take control of such free expression, just as in the USSR and Eastern Bloc. Bodies such as the Union de Escritores y Artistas de Cuba (Cuban Union of Writers and Artists) formed for the various branches of the arts and cultural activities had to be approved by the state. If a writer wanted to publish a book or an artist wanted to stage an exhibition, they had first to get approval from the Cuban government. Many artists and writers including Carlos Franqui left the island to practice their art freely elsewhere.

Many years later, the Peruvian writer, Alfredo Bryce-Echenique (born 1939), said that Che had been one of the main people in government who had been behind the promotion of literature and the arts during this period of Cuban history. He said:

> *In those days, spending fifteen minutes in the presence of Che gave you enormous kudos throughout the Spanish-speaking world.*

JUST A PAWN

Realizing there were some fences to be mended with Cuba, Khrushchev invited Castro to Moscow on April 26, 1963. A plane was sent to pick up Castro's entourage in Havana and they flew to Moscow in complete secrecy, such was the fear that the plane might be shot down. In Russia, the Cuban leader was feted, visiting a number of Soviet cities and being shown military and civilian installations.

At the May Day Parade in Red Square, he stood alongside the principal figures in the government of the USSR and was awarded the Order of Lenin, the Soviet Union's highest civilian decoration. The Russians issued a statement in support of Castro's demand at the United Nations that the Americans withdraw from their naval base at Guantánamo.

However, during private talks at Khrushchev's summer house, Castro learned the real truth that the missiles had been withdrawn from Cuba in exchange for the US missiles being removed from Turkey and Italy.

He was not amused by the idea that Cuba had been just a pawn in the game between the superpowers. Nonetheless, he knew that sticking with the Soviets would help keep him in power. So, he played along.

A CAPITALIST TRICK

Che, on the other hand, was of great concern to Khrushchev who believed him to be leaning too much toward the Chinese, witnessing his disagreements with Moscow on a regular basis. But Che had begun to distrust the Russians long before Cuba was betrayed by Khrushchev during the missile crisis.

Che was suspicious of Russia's stifling bureaucracy and was against motivating workers with money. He believed it was a capitalist trick. He was also extremely disdainful of the privileges the Soviet political elite granted themselves. Even the material sent by the Russians was a disappointment. The tools and equipment never arrived with spare parts, and they rapidly became obsolete.

CHE'S VISION

Che's vision of Marxism and the New Man to take the world forward was different to Marx, Lenin, and Mao Zedong's visions. He was adamant that socialism could not be achieved by employing the methods of capitalism—that is, by financially incentivizing the workforce and seeking profit in their business dealings.

His New Man would not wish to work just to better his material life and acquire things. Rather, he should work hard because he had a moral duty to do so and that in return he and his loved ones would be taken care of by society.

In general Cuba was like Russia, being strangled by a dominant bureaucracy. At his Ministry of Industry, centralization had become the big theme, discouraging initiative and enterprise. The slogans of the state reinforced this message, proclaiming—"war on bureaucratism," "streamline the state apparatus," "production without restraints," and "responsibility for production."

Che worked as frantically as ever. In February 1963, he was driving a cane-cutter for twelve hours a day at a sugar mill. He delivered the closing address at the National Sugar Industry conference in Camagüey. Cuba's industrial and agricultural production was his responsibility and if it meant he had to check every stage of the process to get it going, he would!

CELIA IS ARRESTED

On her return from Europe, Celia was detained by the Argentine customs and then arrested for supposedly smuggling communist propaganda into the country. It was an invented charge of course, but nevertheless she was thrown into a women's prison in Buenos Aires.

Her thoughts may have been diverted from her ordeal slightly by the news of the birth of Che and Aleida's third child, a daughter whom they named Celia in her honor. Even though they could not find Celia guilty of anything, at that time in Argentina, the military could keep her locked up for as long as they wanted without trial.

The de la Sernas and Guevaras pulled as many strings as they could, and got a judge friend to set her free. Before anyone in authority knew what was going on, Celia was safely in Montevideo, Uruguay. Che tried to get her to fly to Havana but she declined his offer, preferring to stay and campaign. Only once the new Argentinean president Arturo Illia had been inaugurated could she cross back to Buenos Aires again from Uruguay.

THE PRICE OF GLORY

While Che was visiting Algiers in July 1963, to celebrate the first anniversary of Algeria gaining independence from

France, the United States declared a complete embargo against Cuba. Later that year all Cuban assets in the United States were frozen.

Around this time, in a speech to a conference of international architecture students Che reiterated where his heart truly lay:

This generation has to pay the price of glory with sacrifice. It has to sacrifice itself day by day to build tomorrow with its efforts ... Your obligations extend beyond the Cuban frontiers; the obligation to spread the ideological flame of the Revolution throughout every corner of the Americas, throughout every corner of the world where our voice is heard.

Che gets a hearty greeting from Algerian Premier Ahmed Ben Bella as he arrives in Algiers on July 4, 1963.

A SHORT HISTORY OF AMERICAN EMBARGOES

● ● ● ● ● ● ● ● ● ●

The first US embargo against Cuba (or "El Bloqueo," the blockade, as it is known in Cuba) was in March 1958 when the USA imposed a ban on arms during the fighting between Castro's rebels and Batista's government troops. The blockade actually had more impact on Batista's men than the rebels whose arms were being supplied by the Soviet Union.

In July 1960, the US cut the amount of sugar it was buying from Cuba which led to the Soviet Union buying the sugar surplus. In October, after Castro had nationalized the US-owned oil refineries in Cuba without compensation, President Eisenhower cancelled the import of Cuban sugar and prohibited the sale of all products to Cuba apart from medicine and food. Castro responded by nationalizing all Cuban-based American businesses and the US then severed diplomatic relations.

After the Bay of Pigs invasion, in September 1961, President Kennedy imposed a complete trade embargo and a ban on aid to Cuba. Then after the Cuban Missile Crisis he froze all Cuban assets in the US.

In March 1977, the restrictions on American citizens traveling to Cuba was allowed to lapse by President Carter but was reinstated by President Reagan in April 1982. The travel ban, however, now applied only to businessmen and tourists. Officials of the US government, researchers, those employed by news or film-making companies or people who had close relatives in Cuba were now free to come and go.

In 2000, in response to lobbying by American farmers, President Clinton relaxed the embargo to allow the sale of agricultural goods and medicine to Cuba for humanitarian reasons. After Hurricane Michelle in 2001, the Cuban government allowed food to be purchased from America. By 2007 the USA was the biggest supplier of food to Cuba and its fifth largest trading partner.

As of 2004, it is not prohibited for US citizens to travel to Cuba, but it is illegal for them to make transactions on the island without a US government license. This effectively makes it impossible for an American tourist to travel to Cuba because they would not be allowed to spend any money and even paying airport taxes on a ticket would mean they were breaking the law.

In 2009, President Barack Obama eased the travel ban permitting Cuban-Americans to fly freely to Cuba and in 2011, missionaries and students were allowed to fly. Then, in 2014 Obama announced a plan to re-establish relations with Cuba. Licenses were granted to establish ferries between Florida and Cuba but the general travel ban remains in place for American citizens.

President Barack Obama and Cuban President Raúl Castro during a joint press conference at the Palace of the Revolution in Havana, Cuba, 2016.

Che during a visit to Algeria.

PART FOUR

¡HASTA LA VICTORIA SIEMPRE!

BETTER TO DIE STANDING
THAN TO LIVE ON YOUR KNEES.
CHE GUEVARA

CHAPTER 13

EXPORTING REVOLUTION

The assassination of President John F. Kennedy in Dallas in November 1963 shocked the entire world. Among the many conspiracy theories was that he had been killed by the Cuban exile community in America who were disappointed about his approach to Cuba. They considered that the dead president had gone soft on Castro. Che intimated that he would not have wanted Kennedy to die because he felt that it was better the devil you know. They understood Kennedy well enough to know how he would react in a given situation.

THE NEXT LEVEL

In Cuba, Che, Raúl and Fidel Castro spent many hours discussing how they could take the Cuban brand of revolution to the next level to bring down other dictatorships around the Caribbean and Latin America. Fidel Castro was not as vocal as Che, but he certainly agreed with the principle. At the 26th of July anniversary in 1960, he swore an oath "to continue making the Fatherland the example that will convert the Cordillera of the Andes into the Sierra Maestra of the American continent."

Che (right) with Fidel (left) and Raúl Castro in Havana.

They began by providing support to exiles from other countries that languished under repressive regimes. But they naively failed to hide their activities and pretty soon word had spread that the new Cuban government was ready to bring down other dictatorships. Before long, Cuba was full of disgruntled Latin American exiles lining up looking for help to start a revolution in their country.

But it was not Castro they needed to ask. Castro had delegated the responsibility to Che, who was very careful not to help anyone that he thought might end up with a capitalist or bourgeois government.

If they did get to see him, they were fortunate indeed, as Che was hardly ever seen in public. This helped sustain the image of the "the legend," and rumors began to fly about this foreigner who had become the leading light of a revolution. There were rumors that he was a Soviet agent working for the Comintern (Communist International) to spread communism worldwide.

DISASTER IN PANAMA

Bordered by Costa Rica to the west and Colombia to the south-east, Panama was originally part of the Republic of Colombia. With the backing of the United States, Panama seceded from Colombia in 1903, allowing the construction of the Panama Canal by the US Army between 1904 and 1914.

But relations between the US and Panama had not been good, and hit a new low in 1956 when the US claimed it had rights of sovereignty over the Panama Canal. In May 1958 a student demonstration against the United States developed into a full-scale riot. The government called out the National Guard and nine died during the violence. The extensive civil unrest made Panama a likely candidate for revolution, and Che decided the Panamanian rebels would be the first deserving cause to be helped by Cuba.

Che and Castro might have believed Panama would be an easy country to overthrow, but in the end it turned out to be far from straightforward. The rebels were transported to a beach in Panama in April 1959, and without putting up much of a fight were swiftly taken prisoner by the well-prepared government troops.

The revolution in Panama was over before it had started. It was a total disaster, with the invasion lasting just a few hours.

DEFEAT IN NICARAGUA

Nicaragua was next. Officially the largest country in Central America, with Honduras to the north, and Costa Rica to the south, the country had been ruled by the repressive and corrupt Somoza family since 1936.

Che and Castro were convinced the people must hate their ruler so much that they would rise up at the first opportunity. The fighting went on for three months but in the end, the rebels were once again defeated.

DOMINICAN WIPE-OUT

The Dominican Republic shares the island of Hispaniola with Haiti. The capital city of Santo Domingo is the the oldest continuously inhabited city in the Americas and the site of the first permanent European settlement, after Christopher Columbus landed on Hispaniola on December 5, 1492.

On June 14, 1959, Cuban guerrillas and Dominican exiles landed at Constanza and Puerto Plata in a two-pronged attempt to overthrow the cruel regime of Generalissimo Rafael Trujillo. The General had been lining his pockets and repressing his people since 1930.

Unfortunately for the rebels, however, Trujillo was an experienced campaigner. He had not been President for thirty years without knowing who his enemies were, and how to deal with them. He found out about the twin invasions in advance and his army was ready. The rebels were wiped out and Trujillo remained in power until he was assassinated in 1961.

Building the Panama Canal

The isthmus connecting North and South America has always looked like a wonderful potential short-cut between the Atlantic and Pacific Oceans. However, it was not until 1881 that French diplomat Ferdinand De Lesseps came up with a plan for a canal to be built.

French engineers soon discovered the De Lesseps proposal was physically impossible to build. However, by the time alternative plans were finally accepted, more than 22,000 workers had perished from malaria, yellow fever, and dysentery. In 1889 the French construction company went bankrupt and in 1893, De Lesseps was arrested and convicted of fraud. He died a year later at age 89.

In 1903, with the support of the United States, Panama revolutionaries declared independence from Colombia, and granted extensive ownership rights to the US for the construction of a canal. By 1913 there was finally a traversable route between the two oceans. In 1914, French crane boat *Alexandre La Valley* made the first passage through the canal which is now used by around 15,000 ships a year.

CHAOS IN HAITI

Occupying the western part of the island of Hispaniola, the native population of Haiti was decimated in 1492 when Columbus arrived. The explorer thought he had found India, but his sailors carried devastating European diseases and the natives died in great numbers.

After François "Papa Doc" Duvalier (1907 – 71) was elected president in 1957, his regime rapidly became totalitarian. Ruling through a mixture of Haitian voodoo myths and personality cult, his undercover death squad enforcers, the Tonton Macoutes, terrorized the people and eliminated Papa Doc's political opponents without hesitation.

On August 14, 1959, a revolutionary force led by Comandante Henry Fuentes landed on the island at Les Irois on Haiti's west coast. Not for the first time their Cuban backers had underestimated the strength of the government army. With neither sufficient men nor arms, the invaders lasted only a few days before surrendering. Their fate was to be grim once they were in the hands of the Tonton Macoutes.

Castro and Che had succeeded only in causing chaos throughout the region. All the old regimes were still firmly in power, while many of the rebel exiles who had come to them for help were dead or rotting in prison.

THE BOLIVIAN INSURGENCY

Having comprehensively failed four times, Castro and Che decided to focus their attention on South America instead, starting with Bolivia. The main vehicle for the overthrow of the Bolivian government was the new Cuban ambassador to Chile, José Tabares del Real.

Tabares del Real traveled extensively across Bolivia trying to encourage the workers and peasants to rise up against the government of Hernan Siles Zuazo. But it was never going to work. President Zuazo had just a few years earlier commanded these same workers and peasants in a social revolution, and he still had their backing.

In 1960, Tabares del Real was expelled from Bolivia for his anti-government activities and his work was carried on by the Cuban Chargé d'Affaires in La Paz, Mauro García Triana. A plan was devised for an armed insurrection in Bolivia. But when the Bolivian government got suspicious, an emergency was declared and 150 communists were immediately arrested.

Documents were found that linked García Triana with the plot to incite "a socialist revolution in Latin America." Che had planned that Bolivia would be the catalyst for a revolution that was going to sweep across the entire continent. But once more his plans had failed.

CHANGING ARGENTINA

In the early days, when Che joined the Cuban rebels in Mexico, Castro had made a promise to him that when the time was right, he would be happy to let Che start a revolution in his homeland. He even promised to help him when that day arrived.

In June 1960, Che began his moves to get involved in changing Argentina when he met three representatives of former President Juan Perón who was at that time in exile. Che had grown up detesting Perón and his regime but he was a pragmatist now, a politician who used whatever means were available to gain his goals. He agreed upon a deal with Perón's men to work with *peronistas* in Argentina to bring down the government.

The government they were trying to overthrow was that of the democratically elected President Arturo Frondizi. Che sought to end US influence in South America, with the installation of a government that would be less compliant to American wishes. He dispatched agents to Argentina with the aim of setting up guerrilla training camps.

TOO DANGEROUS TO GO ON

Raúl Castro's former secretary, Guillermo León Antich, was put in charge of the operation while working as Chargé d'Affaires

FRANÇOIS DUVALIER

François "Papa Doc" Duvalier (1907 – 71) was President of Haiti from 1957 to 1971. Born in Port-au-Prince in 1907, the son of a justice of the peace, he completed a degree in medicine from the University of Haiti in 1934. His expertise as a physician contributed to his nickname "Papa Doc."

Elected president in 1957 on a populist and black nationalist platform, Duvalier was very much aware of the political power of the poor, uneducated black majority. He strengthened his support by using elements of Haitian mythology with ceremonies of music, dance, and spirit possession.

After thwarting a military *coup d'état* in 1958, he eliminated any opposition with his own personal police force, the Tonton Macoutes. Estimates of those killed are as high as 60,000. He was re-elected unopposed as President for Life in 1964.

Duvalier fostered a cult of personality and claimed that he was the physical embodiment of Baron Samedi, one of the *loa* spirits of Haitian Vodou. He often wore sunglasses in order to hide his eyes and talked with the strong nasal tone associated with the *loa*. Unlike saints or angels, however, the *loa* do not help those in need, they are there to be served.

During the 1960s Duvalier became increasingly paranoid, keeping the head of former enemy Blucher Philogenes as a trophy in his closet, and believing another political enemy was able to change into a black dog. He instructed the Tonton Macoutes to kill all black dogs on sight.

Duvalier died in April 1971, at age 64, from heart disease and diabetes. His 19-year-old son Jean-Claude Duvalier, nicknamed "Baby Doc," succeeded him as president.

in Buenos Aires, but documents intercepted in Montevideo revealed the plans to the Argentine authorities. Two guerrilla training camps were raided in July 1961. A Cuban army trainer was arrested, and copious amounts of Cuban propaganda discovered, including Che's *Guerrilla Warfare*.

Unfortunately, the Cuban embassy officials defected but were persuaded by Miami-based anti-Castro exiles that they would be more useful if they remained in their posts to gather evidence on what Che and Castro were up to. They managed to hold out until August 1961 when it became too dangerous to go on, and they resigned, asking for political asylum in Argentina.

CHE'S SECRET VISIT

It was during this time that Che was secretly invited to Argentina by Frondizi to discuss Cuban-American relations. While Frondizi wanted to act as a mediator on the world stage, he clearly did not understand that Che was working behind the scenes to overthrow the Argentine government.

Che came and went before the army even knew he had been in Argentina. Much to the fury of the generals who would have dearly loved to get some answers from the rebel leader to some very difficult questions.

Then in September, more documents were published that showed plainly the murky machinations of Cuba in Argentina,

SOUTH AMERICA'S PRINCIPAL CASH CROP

• • • • • • • • • •

Coca is known throughout the world as the main ingredient of one of the world's most lucrative products, the psychoactive drug cocaine. For 35 years, the international cocaine trade has made South American drug cartels rich and helped fund guerrilla groups such as the FARC in Colombia whose violence has plagued the country.

Because US farmers receive substantial government subsidies for products such as corn and maize to keep prices low, developing countries in the south find it impossible to compete. In such a system, illicit crops became one of the only ways for many farmers to make a decent living. So coca is grown as a cash crop in Argentina, Bolivia, Colombia, Ecuador, and Peru.

Peasant farmers need the income from coca simply to support their families. A fundamental part of the way of life, coca has been farmed by generations of farmers in the Andes, with the leaves being chewed for centuries by the natives as a stimulant and a source of energy.

contributing to Cuba's expulsion from the Organization of American States (OAS) the following year.

THE CAT IS OUT OF THE BAG

Evidence that the Cuban embassy officials gathered was released just a month after Che's meeting with Arturo Frondizi. The documents showed clearly Che was in charge of Cuban-Argentinean relations, and had established a far-reaching network penetrating Argentinean politics, the government, the military, the media, and the universities. It was all intended to benefit Juan Perón and his supporters.

More evidence went on to describe how Che had established the secret guerrilla training schools within Argentina, while he tried to unite the Peronists and the left in a revolutionary movement. Further documents proved it was all part of a propaganda initiative directed against the United States and its influence in the region.

Che's agents were shown to be controlling activities on the Argentinean borders with Paraguay and Bolivia, linking them to the coca drug smugglers who caused constant trouble for the government forces.

The cat was well and truly out of the bag. Che was back, and the government troops went onto full-scale alert.

GOING BACK TO ARGENTINA

Che's visit to the presidential palace in Buenos Aires was the final straw for the Arturo Frondizi regime. He was unceremoniously kicked out of office by the Army, and banished into exile on the island of Martín García. Argentina broke off all diplomatic relations with Cuba, and Cuba was thrown out of the OAS. Che's network, based in the Cuban embassy in Buenos Aires, was totally demolished. He had failed to export revolution to his homeland.

It was not the end, however. Che tried again, this time working with Jorge Ricardo Masetti, a fellow Argentinean adventurer and a *peronista*.

In 1959, Che had invited Masetti to Cuba to establish a news agency, Prensa Latina, that would function as a government mouthpiece. The aim was to diminish the influence of American news agencies and spread Cuban propaganda in the Latin American media. Masetti's position did not last long, however.

Masetti quickly made many enemies among the Communists and Cuban journalists. He held the same views as Che that the armed struggle was the only way to defeat totalitarian regimes. When Che suggested he lead a revolutionary struggle in his homeland, Masetti did not need asking twice.

Harvesting coca leaves in Bolivia. The oldest man ever recorded, 123-year-old Carmelo Flores Laura from Bolivia, claimed his astonishing age was due to his daily coca leaf chewing.

TEAM BUILDING

Ciro Bustos, an Argentinean painter from Mendoza, came to Cuba in 1962 with his wife. He joined Che's team and underwent guerrilla training with Federico Mendez, another Argentinean and two other men—"Leonardo" and "Miguel." Hermes Peña Torres, one of Che's bodyguards joined them too.

Che made regular visits to the training camp to check on their progress, often accompanied by Masetti and Comandante Manuel Piñeiro who was Cuban Head of Intelligence and his deputy, Juan Carretero, known as "Ariel."

The group were complemented by the head of police in Havana, Abelardo "Furry" Colome-Ibarra, who would be responsible for looking after the base and for communications with Havana. They were trained by a man who had fought in the Spanish Civil War, whose real name was Francisco Ciutat but who went under the pseudonym "Ángel Martínez." Ciro Bustos was given responsibility for security and intelligence, Miguel was given logistics, and Leonardo was the doctor.

KEEPING A LOW PROFILE

They were embedded into a battalion of Cuban troops to give them some experience of army life, and then sent to Europe so they could keep a low profile. They flew to Prague and stayed at an empty hotel at Lake Slapy, posing as Cuban scholarship students. Weeks passed and Masetti became tired of waiting.

He flew to Algiers to ask permission to travel there from President Ahmed Ben Bella and Defense Minister Houari Boumedienne. Arriving via Paris, they moved into a villa on the outskirts of Algiers. It gave them an opportunity to see a new revolutionary government in operation. They were accompanied by armed security men whenever they left the confines of the villa, but mainly continued their military training.

Back in Havana, Che spent a couple of months quizzing his old friend Ricardo Rojo for information about the volatile political situation in Argentina. Perón's party had been banned but he continued to influence matters from his Spanish exile.

Che with Jorge Ricardo Masetti, 1959.

THE PEOPLES' GUERRILLA ARMY

Masetti and his men traveled to southern Bolivia in June 1963 on Algerian diplomatic passports, basing themselves at a farm near the Argentine border and continued their training. Their weapons followed them to Latin America in Algerian diplomatic bags.

They gave themselves a name, the Ejercito Guerrillero del Pueblo (EGP) which translates as the Peoples' Guerrilla Army. The plan was to create a *foco insurrectional* which meant that Masetti did not have to liaise with any other groups, leftist or communist. Rather, with just his small band, he would become the focus of a popular uprising.

This was undoubtedly a mistake, and one that Che repeated in later revolutionary efforts. It also ignored Che's dictum that if a country had a democratically elected government, then it was not the best place to start a guerrilla war. Argentina's Arturo Illia had been elected by the majority of the people, and the army had now taken a back seat.

COMANDANTE SEGUNDO

Calling himself "Comandante Segundo," Masetti and his band of guerrillas slipped over the border into Argentina in two groups at the beginning of September and in December. The fact that he was the "second comandante" suggested that there was a first one, undoubtedly Che, who would probably join them at some point.

The second group was headed by "Captain Hermes" which was the *nom de guerre* chosen by Hermes Peña. The area for their activity included the provinces of Jujuy and Salta, both of which Che had cycled through as a young man.

Arriving on Argentine soil, Masetti at first wanted to abandon the initiative as he thought there was little chance of a popular uprising. He even sent messages out across the country to that effect. But he had second thoughts when he realized that the poor people who would normally vote for Perón now effectively had no voice. Many of them had spoiled their ballot papers or left them blank in the election rather than vote for Arturo Illia.

IN THE MOUNTAINS AND JUNGLES

Masetti's behavior became unaccountably erratic and his treatment of his men in the mountains and jungles of northern Argentina was harsh. One young man was not ready for the rigors of the guerrilla lifestyle, and was unable to keep up on the marches. Instead of simply dismissing him, Masetti court-martialled him and sentenced him to death.

The *coup de grace* was delivered by Ciro Bustos. Another new recruit was executed for not being able to handle the situation while another absconded. Bustos later described the group as "nothing but deluded dreamers."

Masetti issued a call to arms to the people of Argentina, published in a *peronista* magazine. Undoubtedly, this only served to forewarn the government that revolutionary guerrillas were in the country. As things began to unravel further, the group was infiltrated by two undercover police officers who guided the authorities to their location.

THE MOST SILENT DEFEAT

On April 18, 1964, it was announced on the radio that the guerrillas had been dispersed. Hermes Peña and Jorge Guille were killed in the police ambush, while the others went into hiding. For days they tried to survive on a hillside without any food, but three of them died in their sleep of starvation. Another fell from a cliff.

Masetti and 23-year-old Oscar Atilio Altamirano were never seen again, in all likelihood they died of starvation in the jungle. Both Ciro Bustos and "Furry" Colome-Ibarra somehow made it back to Cuba. Those guerrillas who were captured or who surrendered were tried, and given long sentences ranging from 5 to 15 years.

All evidence of this doomed escapade was totally removed from the official archives in Cuba, and faded away as if it had never existed. As Che's erstwhile traveling companion Ricardo Rojo wrote:

> *The tragedy of "Comandante Segundo" in the mountains and jungles of northern Argentina was the most silent guerrilla defeat in Latin America. It received little publicity in the press, and even leftist publications feared compromising themselves with an adventure in which, many believed, were seen traces of provocation organized by the intelligence services.*

BROTHERS IN BATTLE

While his plans for revolution in Argentina were falling apart, Che continued with his ministerial life in Cuba. A Week of Solidarity with the people of South Vietnam was celebrated in December 1963, and Che rounded off the week with a speech in the capital, saying:

> *We hail our brothers in South Vietnam as brothers in battle, as a fellow example in these difficult moments in world history, and even more, as our allies, as front-line soldiers, in the front trenches of the world proletariat against imperialism.*

Then in 1964 he kicked off the year with a reception at the Palace of the Revolution, followed by a huge rally in Revolution Square the next day. It was the fifth anniversary of the Cuban Revolution.

In the first month of the year, he was in talks with representatives of the USSR, signing a technical aid deal with them. At the end of that month he traveled with Castro to a farm at Oro de Guisa where they inspected some new machines for cutting sugar cane. The

Fidel Castro at a Russian winter celebration in Moscow, 1964.

news on the sugar front was good following a trip Castro had taken to Moscow during which the Soviets agreed to buy almost all the Cuban sugar crop at a price higher than the market value. The Russians were still anxious to keep Cuba in their camp. Sadly, however, there was no support for Che's ideas about the industrialization of Cuba or the diversification of its agriculture.

BLOOD ON THEIR HANDS

At the beginning of February 1964, Che flew his Cessna plane to Guanahacabibes to inspect a re-education center he had established there for officials who had committed offenses. They could go there voluntarily to better understand the revolution and how their acts undermined its progress. After they had amended their thinking they were permitted to return to their posts and their record would contain no mention of their correctional treatment.

In the middle of March, he traveled to Geneva to attend a United Nations Conference on Trade and Development. He delivered a passionate speech to the conference in plenary session, in which he said:

> It must be clearly understood, and we say it in all frankness, that the only way to solve the problems now besetting humanity is to eliminate completely the exploitation of dependent countries by developed capitalist countries, with all the consequences that implies ... Just as it is the case that current prices are unjust, it is also the case that these prices are conditioned by the monopolistic limitation of markets and the establishment of political relations which give "competition" a purely one-sided meaning—freedom of competition for the monopolies, a free fox among the "free" chickens.

In the speech, Che challenged the conference for not inviting East Germany, North Vietnam, and North Korea to attend, pointing out that apartheid South Africa was present.

He went on to accuse the United Nations of having blood on their hands over the death of the Prime Minister of the Congo, Patrice Lumumba, who had been assassinated even though he had been seeking the protection of the UN peacekeeping force in the Congo.

FEEL THE ELECTRICITY

Che was giving speeches and the world was listening, but in a private conversation with the Argentine Ambassador to the United Nations, he expressed his desire to get involved in the armed struggle against oppression once more.

His interest may have also been aroused by a woman named Tamara Bunke Bider. She had just finished a counter-espionage course, organized by the Head of Cuban Intelligence Manuel Piñeiro. Che was sending her to scout for information in Bolivia, where they planned a guerrilla-led insurgency to inspire revolution throughout South America.

In mid-August, Che proudly received a communist work certificate for the 240 hours of voluntary work he had completed in the first half of 1964. He had great faith in voluntary work. It fitted with his view of how society should function and with his vision of the New Man.

A few weeks before this event, Che had attended a reception for Switzerland's National Day at the Swiss embassy. An American journalist, Lyle Stuart who was there described the evening:

> Dozens of people stood chatting, cocktails in hand. My back was to the entrance but I knew, without looking, that Che had arrived for you could literally feel the electricity. It's one of those things you had to experience to understand. He was charged with magnetism and charm and strength, and—yes, beauty. I.F. Stone (the American investigative journalist) once described him as "the most beautiful man I ever met."

TAMARA BUNKE BIDER

Known as "Tania the Guerrilla," Tamara Bunke Bider was an Argentine-born, East German communist revolutionary. She was born in 1937 in Buenos Aires, daughter of two German communists, Erich Bunke and Nadia Bider who had been forced to flee Germany when the Nazis came to power in 1933.

In 1952, the family returned to East Germany, settling in Stalinstadt. She studied political science at Humboldt University, East Berlin, and joined the youth wing of the Socialist Unity Party of Germany, the Free German Youth (FGY) as well as the World Federation of Democratic Youth. As a result of her linguistic abilities— she could speak Russian, English, Spanish, and German—and her keen interest in Latin America, she found work as a translator in the International Department of the FGY.

She first met Che in 1960, acting as his interpreter during his visit to Leipzig as part of a Cuban trade delegation. She was 23 years old, and Che was already a man she worshipped as a hero. Then in 1961, inspired by Che and the Cuban Revolution, she went to live in Cuba, working for the Ministry of Education and the Federation of Cuban Women.

She was selected for Che's expedition to Bolivia to spark insurrection all across Latin America. She was trained in self-defense, how to use weapons, and how to send coded messages by radio transmission. She adopted the name "Tania" as her *nom de guerre*.

Tania proved useful in Bolivia, sending messages to Castro in Havana and also to Che and his men in the jungle. Eventually, however, her cover was blown and she had no option but to join Che and his men. There have been rumors since then that Tania and Che became lovers but it was never confirmed.

She was shot dead on August 31, 1967, by CIA-assisted Bolivian Army Rangers while wading across the Río Grande at Vado del Yeso with her rifle held above her head. Her body was carried downstream and recovered by the Bolivian Army on September 6. Castro proclaimed her "a hero of the Cuban Revolution."

There have been many rumors that Tania was actually a spy for the Russian KGB or the East German Stasi secret police, on a mission to kill Che. But both organizations deny it. Still another rumor suggests she was carrying Che's child when she was killed, but there is no evidence to support this claim either.

CHAPTER 14

SPREADING THE WORD

The United States persevered with its efforts to maintain the perception of Cuba as an outcast to the international community. Brazil and Bolivia had both severed diplomatic relations.

ON THE RED SQUARE PODIUM

Che headed for Moscow in October 1964 to represent Cuba at the celebrations marking the 47th anniversary of the 1917 Russian Revolution. Despite his poor relations with the Soviet hierarchy, the visit went well and Che was able to get to know the new Soviet leader, Leonid Brezhnev (1906 – 82) who had replaced Khrushchev at the top.

He stood on the viewing podium in Red Square to watch the customary march-past. Later, alongside the first man in space Yuri Gagarin, he hosted the opening of Friendship House, a meeting place for people from Cuba and Russia.

Meanwhile, he felt increasingly frustrated, expressing to his friend Alberto Granado how bad he had felt sending Masetti and his men to their deaths while he sat behind a desk shuffling papers. He must have been considering even then leaving Cuba and trying to spread revolution around the world. In a speech after his return from the USSR, he said:

Cuba's name is the emblem of what can be achieved by the revolutionary struggle and the belief that the world can be a better place; it is the ideal for which it is worth risking one's life, even unto death, on the battlefields of every continent in the world.

A PATRIOT OF LATIN AMERICA

On December 11, 1964, Che addressed the United Nations at the 19th Annual General Assembly where all member states have equal representation. He ended with rousing words of revolution:

For this great mass of humanity has said, "Enough!" and has begun to march. And their march of giants will not be halted until they conquer their true independence—for which they have vainly died more than once. Today, however, those who die will die like the Cubans at Playa Girón. They will die for their own true and never-to-be-surrendered independence.

It was a call to arms to the young men of Latin America, the Third World, and the Non-Aligned countries, saying that enough was enough and it was time to rise up. Finally, someone was saying what they felt on the world stage.

Naturally, his words received a hostile reception and a number of Latin American countries spoke against him, as did Adlai Stevenson of the United States. Having the right of reply, Che stood up once again. Apologizing for speaking a second time, he said:

I am a patriot of Latin America and of all Latin American countries. Whenever necessary I would be ready to lay down my life for the liberation of any Latin American country, without asking anything from anyone, without demanding anything, without exploiting anyone. And this is not just the frame of mind of the individual addressing this assembly at present; it is the frame of mind of the entire Cuban people.

ESTABLISHING GOOD RELATIONS

While he was in New York, ABC's UN correspondent Lisa Howard invited him to her apartment to meet Democratic Senator Eugene McCarthy who was an opponent of America's involvement in Southeast Asia. McCarthy later said that Che told him he was interested in establishing a trading relationship with the United States, but when McCarthy passed word to President Lyndon Johnson, the president was not interested.

Che did not return to Cuba after New York. Instead, he traveled via Canada and Ireland to Africa. He spent three months visiting Algeria, Mali, Congo-Brazzaville, Guinea, Dahomey, Tanzania, and Egypt. He visited his old friend President Ahmed Ben Bella in Algeria where he established a base for his various visits. It was an interesting time in Africa, many countries having gained independence from the colonial powers in recent years and Che's task was to develop friendships with them.

THE ARMED STRUGGLE

Che also met the leaders of revolutionary movements who were still engaged in the armed struggle for power, men such as Agostinho Neto, leader of the People's Movement for the Liberation of Angola (MPLA). Che established a relationship between Cuba and Angola that would last for thirty years, and Neto eventually became the first President of Angola.

He also met Amílcar Cabral, leader of the movement to free Guinea-Bissau from Portuguese rule. The Portuguese were eager to hold on to Guinea-Bissau because they felt that were it to achieve independence then Angola would follow and it was rich in oil reserves.

Che had considerable respect for Cabral, who also believed in the armed struggle. But Cabral did not seek men or weapons from Cuba, believing the people of his nation should fight for their own freedom. He did however ask for teachers, doctors, nurses, technicians, and medical supplies.

Che and Lisa Howard smoking cigars together during their New York meeting, 1964.

REVOLUTION IN THE CONGO

It became very obvious in the 1950s that things were changing rapidly in Africa. If the Europeans were to maintain influence in the region, they would have to build relationships with the new black leaders who were emerging and who could be bought and bribed into bending to the will of their former colonial masters. In the new Republic of the Congo, however, that was not to be. Patrice Lumumba, the country's first prime minister was not a man who could be bought. Educated and decent, he was loved by the Congolese.

Immediately after the Republic of the Congo gained independence on June 30, 1960, Congolese troops mutinied and Katanga, a province rich in minerals such as cobalt, copper, and uranium, ceded from the republic under the leadership of businessman and politician Moïse Tshombe.

Things went from bad to worse when, in September 1960, Colonel Joseph-Désiré Mobutu, backed by the United States and Belgium, mounted a coup against Lumumba's government. The civil war in the country grew, and white mercenaries began to arrive from South Africa, recruited by the British-Irish mercenary leader, Michael "Mad Mike" Hoare.

The CIA sent some of the Cuban exiles who had suffered such an ignominious defeat at the Bay of Pigs to help. Lumumba was assassinated by Belgian and Katangan officers on January 17, 1961. The UN troops who had been sent to provide protection for him simply looked the other way while the murder was carried out.

THE CONGO FREE STATE

● ● ● ● ● ● ● ● ● ● ●

During the "Scramble for Africa" in the late nineteenth century, when European powers carved up Africa into colonies for themselves, the central African territory known as the Congo was claimed by King Leopold II of Belgium (1835 – 1909). It was a private project that was under his sole ownership although the Belgian government "loaned" him the money.

The king commissioned the famous explorer, Henry Morton Stanley (1841 – 1904) as his agent on a five-year contract to explore the Congo and establish a colony. The Congo Free State was established on February 5, 1885, under the personal rule of Leopold and his private army, the Force Publique.

Leopold plundered the natural resources of the Congo, amassing a vast personal fortune in the process. It was driven by the global demand for rubber and intensive work began on extracting the sap from rubber trees. Slave labor of the native population was used to keep up with demand, and beatings, torture, killing, and mutilation were common punishment when quotas were not achieved.

It has been estimated that as many as 15 million people may have died during this period, although it is impossible to be accurate. Eventually, in 1908 the Belgian parliament responded to international condemnation of human rights abuse by compelling Leopold to pass over the Congo Free State to Belgium, making it a Belgian colony, known as the Belgian Congo. Leopold died in 1909 without ever setting foot in the Congo.

Leopold II of Belgium.

AHMED BEN BELLA

Born in Maghnia, western Algeria, Ahmed Ben Bella (1916 – 2012) was an Algerian socialist revolutionary. The son of a farmer and small businessman, he studied at the French school in Maghnia before attending school in Tlemcen, where he experienced for the first time the discrimination shown by Europeans toward native Algerians.

He volunteered for the French Army in 1936 and fought for France during World War II, earning the Croix de Guerre. After the fall of France, he joined a Moroccan infantry regiment and was again decorated for bravery at Monte Cassino, Italy.

He returned to Algeria after the war and became active in the opposition to the French colonial regime. Eventually after being arrested and serving eight years in prison he joined the revolutionaries of the Front de Liberation Nationale (FLN).

During the Algerian War between the FLN and France, Ben Bella played an important role, and there were several attempts on his life. Arrested by the French in October 1956,

he remained in prison until 1962, but following Algeria's eventual independence from France, his popularity increased.

On September 20, 1962, he was elected prime minister. He nationalized the land in foreign hands but introduced a one-party state, something with which the majority of Algerians seemed to have little problem. On September 15, 1963, he was elected the first President of Algeria, unopposed. He introduced many reforms, becoming more socialist in his policies.

After Algeria was defeated by Morocco in the conflict known as the Sand War, Ben Bella's position became difficult, and in June 1965, he was deposed. After being imprisoned for eight months, Ben Bella spent 14 years under house arrest. In 1979, restrictions on him were eased and he lived in exile in France and Switzerland. He returned to Algeria in 1991 to found a new political party, but it was banned in 1997. He died in 2012, at age 96, after respiratory illnesses. Algeria declared eight days of national mourning.

n policemen arrest Algerian political rebel
Ahmed Ben Bella in Algiers, 1956.

AMILCAR CABRAL

Amílcar Lopes de Costa Cabral (1924 – 1973) was one of the leading African thinkers of the twentieth century. An activist, agronomist, and nationalist leader, he helped lead the west African state of Guinea-Bissau to independence from Portugal.

Born in Bafatá, Guinea-Bissau, to wealthy Cape Verdean parents, Cabral was educated in Cape Verde and studied agronomy at university in Lisbon, where he helped start student movements opposed to Portuguese colonialism.

Returning to Africa in the 1950s, he became heavily involved in the struggle for independence for Portugal's African colonies. He founded the Partido Africano da Independência da Guiné e Cabo Verde (PAIGC) and helped Agostinho Neto to found the Movimento Popular de Libertação de Angola (MPLA).

As leader of the PAIGC's guerrilla force from 1963, he realized that victory could only be won if his troops learned to live off the land alongside the rest of the population. They taught the farmers improved techniques so they could feed not only their own family and members of their tribe, but also the soldiers of the PAIGC. He also established a trade-and-barter system whereby goods were sold at better prices than were offered by colonial store-owners. He established a mobile hospital that cared not only for wounded PAIGC troops but also the local population.

Having captured large areas of the country from the Portuguese, in 1972 Cabral began to assemble a government creating a People's Assembly. But before full independence was gained, he was shot and killed on January 20, 1973, by a disgruntled former rival.

Following his assassination, around a hundred officers and soldiers of the PAIGC who were said to be involved were executed. Cabral's half-brother, Luís (1931 – 2009), assumed leadership of the PAIGC and became the first president of Guinea-Bissau in September 1973.

THE AFRICAN SICKNESS

In his speech at the United Nations in 1964, Che condemned Belgium for its activities in the Congo in 1961. He demanded revenge for the murder of Lumumba. In 1965, when he returned to Algiers, Che declared that after visiting several African countries he felt that:

> *Africa was sick; now it is convalescent and it is getting better. Its sickness was colonialism, its risk of relapse is neo-colonialism.*

He flew to Paris for twenty-four hours before taking a flight to Tanzania where he was met by the Tanzanian President Julius Nyerere. However, he stopped off en route in Brazzaville, capital of the Republic of the Congo. This part of the Congo was known as the Brazzaville Republic to distinguish it from the Democratic Republic of the Congo which was also known as Kinshasa Republic.

THE COMMON FRONT

President Alphonse Massamba-Débat of the Kinshasa Republic had recently proclaimed his country to be a socialist one-party state, that party being his own Mouvement National de la Revolution. His government was at the time providing support for a left-wing uprising that had broken out in the Kinshasa Republic. Massamba-Débat's objective was the unification of the two Congo Republics into one socialist state.

Massamba-Débat wanted the revolution to spread from the Congo to the rest of central Africa and then onward to the north and south. These ideas were, of course, music to Che's ears, especially as Massamba-Débat wanted the Cuban government to help him.

Che passed through Guinea, Ghana, Dahomey, and Algeria, to get to Dar es Salaam, capital of Tanzania, to covertly meet

Che Guevara with Mao Zedong (left) and Zhou Enlai (right) in Beijing, China, 1965.

the Kinshasa leaders—Gaston Soumialot and Laurent Kabila of the the People's Liberation Army or PLA.

He extricated himself from his entourage and the press to inspect the PLA bases in the eastern part of the Congo. Around this time, he came up with the idea of a tricontinental "common front" which he shared with the world. As he left Dar es Salaam, he told the media:

> After completing my tour of seven African countries, I am convinced that it is possible to create a common front to fight against colonialism, imperialism and neo-colonialism.

MEN OF SIMILAR CIRCUMSTANCE

He returned to Algeria and then passed through Cairo en route to Beijing where he spent a week being introduced to high-ranking ministers. He was particularly delighted when Chinese premier Zhou Enlai (1898 – 1976) turned up to a meeting.

Che and Zhou Enlai were men of similar circumstance, and they got on very well together, which is likely to have benefited Cuba's relationship with China. The recent tension between the Soviet Union and China made things difficult. But the Chinese were the principal arms suppliers to Kabila and Soumialot's PLA and were, therefore, even more important to Che.

WITHOUT QUARTER AGAINST THE WORLD

In February 1965, Che spoke at the Organization of Afro-Asian Solidarity, criticizing the USSR and other socialist countries who, in his view, still exploited their people. He called for socialist peoples to work more closely together to help developing countries:

> ... the socialist countries must help pay for the development of countries now starting out on the road to liberation. We state it this way

> with no intention whatsoever of blackmail or dramatics, nor are we looking for an easy way to get closer to the Afro-Asian peoples; it is our profound conviction. Socialism cannot exist without a change in consciousness ... with regard to all peoples suffering from imperialist oppression.

He ended by paying tribute to his friend Ahmed Ben Bella and Algeria where the conference was being staged:

> Few settings from which to make this declaration are as symbolic as Algiers, one of the most heroic capitals of freedom. May the magnificent Algerian people—schooled as few others in sufferings for independence, under the decisive leadership of its party, headed by our dear compañero Ahmed Ben Bella—serve as an inspiration to us in this fight without quarter against world imperialism.

It was no less than Che's revolutionary thesis for the Third World and explained how to integrate the struggle for national determination with socialist ideas. It set the world talking and history has proved him to be right.

SEEING THE FUTURE

He next traveled to the United Arab Republic where he remained from March 3 to 12 with President Gamal Abdel Nasser, visiting factories and talking to workers. It is said that during their conversations, Nasser was particularly surprised by how often Che talked of death. He said during one conversation:

> The turning point in each man's life is the moment in which he decides to face death. If he faces death, then he is a hero whether he becomes a success or not.

Then, on the last day of his extended visit, Che said he hoped to find "a place to fight for world revolution and to accept the challenge of death." As if he could see the future, and knew what lay ahead for him.

Dressed in military fatigues and smoking a cigar, Che reclines in his chair as he appears on the CBS current affairs program *Face the Nation* in New York, December 1964.

CHAPTER 15

CONFLICT IN THE CONGO

Che arrived back in Cuba on March 14, 1965. While he had been in Algiers in February, Aleida had given birth to their fourth child, a boy they decided to call Ernesto. Meanwhile, Che wrote to his mother to let her know that Aleida had undergone a procedure to ensure she would be having no more children.

It may have been concern about her health that necessitated this, but Che undoubtedly already knew that he was going away sometime soon and that it would be foolhardy to have another child.

TAKING REVOLUTION TO THE CONGO

On his return, it is reported, he spent a full twenty-four hours closeted with Raúl and Fidel Castro, briefing them on what he had discovered during his three months away from Cuba. One thing they must have talked about was the Congo. Around 150 men had been undergoing intensive guerrilla training in Cuba before Che had left for Africa.

At the time, no one, not even the Congolese, knew that the Cuban guerrillas would be putting their training into practice in the Congo. They were to be called military instructors as Cuba did not want to be seen as a foreign intruder in an African conflict. The men had all volunteered for the project and all were Afro-Cubans, all that is except Che and his head of intelligence, José María Martínez-Tamayo.

At last Che had found his *cause célèbre*, the venture that would permit him to cover himself with still more revolutionary glory and cement his reputation as a great guerrilla leader. It would also enable him to spread the revolution. He wanted to change the world and the Congo provided a chance to do just that.

TWO BIRDS WITH ONE STONE

Castro wanted to change the world too, and while he was undoubtedly very interested in Africa, the Congo provided him with something else he had been looking for. Never quite able to equal Che's glamorous rock star looks or the twinkling eyes, Castro was jealous of the way the world seemed to admire Che.

The Congo gave Castro a chance not only to forge links with Africa but at the same time to rid himself of any potential threat Che posed to the Cuban leadership. It was the set of circumstances he had been waiting for—to kill two birds with one stone.

Castro had been making strenuous efforts to cultivate the friendship of African revolutionaries, training them and supplying them, but also establishing trade and cultural relations with a number of African countries. History shows that many Cuban citizens had African slaves as ancestors and greater links with Africa would be viewed very favorably by them.

He was also anxious, after the failures in Latin America of recent years, to re-establish his country's revolutionary credentials. Perhaps then the Latin American countries suffering under dictatorships and military rule might take Cuba's attempts to foment revolution more seriously.

Ultimately, the Cuban leader had nothing to lose. On the one hand, neither Cuba nor

Che (right) when he was Cuban Minister of Industry returns to Havana after having made several trips in Asia and Africa. Welcoming him are from left to right: Fidel Castro, Aleida March, Carlos Rafael Rodriguez, and President Osvaldo Dorticós.

Castro would be damaged if Che failed in Africa. On the other hand if Che succeeded, then both Cuba and Castro would come out of it very well indeed.

BLACK MAGIC AND TRIBAL RIVALRIES

Africa seemed a better bet than Latin America for the creation of the "Many Vietnams" Che sought. The logistics were better as African rebels could more easily be supplied by Russia, China, the United Arab Republic, or Algeria. It was also further away from the United States than Latin America and might not draw as much attention from the Americans.

As before, Che sought to create a *foco* to attract guerrillas from the region and even from neighboring countries to the conflict. Hopefully, after the Congo was liberated, these rebels would then return to their homelands to use the experience they had gained in the Congo to liberate their countries.

But there were issues in the Congo that were unique to that part of the world. Deep-rooted tribal rivalries meant that recruits from different tribes would not fight together or support one another. The Congo is composed of numerous tribes of various ethnicities with different beliefs, and speaking different languages. The local belief in black magic did not help the turbulent situation.

Che had been in Havana for only three weeks before he left for Tanzania in full disguise. He was, after all, one the most famous people in the world. He told the men traveling with him to the Congo, to be prepared for a campaign lasting twenty years. He left a tape recording of some poems by Pablo Neruda for Aleida, telling her that when things were right he would send for her.

When Che disappeared from view, the world became curious as to where he might have gone. Asked by an inquisitive reporter where he was, Castro replied:

All I can tell you is that Comandante Guevara is always where he can be most useful to the revolution, and that relations between him and myself are excellent.

CHE'S FAREWELL LETTERS

• • • • • • • • • • •

MANY COMRADES FALL

Che had bade farewell to Castro in an extraordinary letter he wrote in the weeks before he left. In stripping himself of all positions and connections to Cuba, it has been said that he allowed Castro to be free of any blame if all failed and he died in the process. In the letter he said:

In a revolution one triumphs or dies (if it is a real one). Many comrades fall along the way to victory. Today everything has a less dramatic tone, because we are more mature, but the event repeats itself. I feel that I have fulfilled that part of my duty that tied me to the Cuban Revolution in its territory, and I say goodbye to you, to the comrades, to your people, who now are mine. I formally resign my positions in the leadership of the Party, my post as minister, my rank of comandante, and my Cuban citizenship. Nothing legal binds me to Cuba ...

I have lived magnificent days, and at your side I felt the pride of belonging to our people in the brilliant yet sad days of the Caribbean crisis. Seldom has a statesman been more brilliant than you in those days. I am also proud of having followed you without hesitation, identified with your way of thinking and of seeing and appraising dangers and principles. Other nations of the world call for my modest efforts.

I can do that which is denied you because of your responsibility at the head of Cuba, and the time has come for us to part ... I free Cuba from any responsibility, except that which stems from its example. If my final hour finds me under other skies, my last thought will be of this people and especially of you ... I am not ashamed that I leave nothing material to my children and my wife; I am happy it is that way. I ask nothing for them, as the state will provide them with enough to live and have an education.

Hasta la Victoria Siempre! Patria o Muerte!

I embrace you with all my revolutionary fervor.

Che

THE PRODIGAL SON

He wrote other letters to his children and to his parents. To Celia and Ernesto, his parents, he wrote:

Viejos,

Once again I feel beneath my heels the ribs of Rocinante. Once more, I'm on the road with my shield on my arm. Many will call me an adventurer, and that I am—only one of a different sort: one who risks his skin to prove his truths ...

I have loved you very much, only I have not known how to express my affection. I am extremely rigid in my actions, and I think that sometimes you did not understand me. It was not easy to understand me. Nevertheless, please believe me today. Now a willpower that I have polished with an artist's delight will sustain some shaky legs and some weary lungs ... big hug from your obstinate and prodigal son, Che

It was too late for Celia, however. By the time the letter arrived she had died of the cancer from which she had been suffering.

BE GOOD REVOLUTIONARIES

To his children, he wrote that they should grow up to be good revolutionaries, that they should study hard and master technology:

Dear Hildita, Aleidita, Camilo, Celia and Ernesto,

If you read this letter one day, it will mean that I am no longer alive. You will hardly remember me, and the smallest among you will have entirely forgotten me.

Your father was a man who acted as he thought best and who has been absolutely faithful to his convictions. Grow up into good revolutionaries. Study hard to master technique, which gives you mastery over nature. Remember that it is the Revolution which is important and that each of us, taken in isolation, is worth nothing. Above all be sensitive, in the deepest areas of yourselves, to any injustice committed against whoever it may be anywhere in the world.

Yours always, my children. I hope to see you again.

A big strong kiss from Daddy.

Che with Aleida March and their children. Left to right: Ernesto (born 1965), Camilo (born 1962), Aleida (born 1960), and Celia (born 1963).

THE PASSING OF CELIA DE LA SERNA

In 1965, Celia became ill again. Her cancer recurred and, realizing that she did not have much time left, she wrote to her son asking if she could spend some time with him. She kept the seriousness of her condition from him and Che wrote back to say she could not come as he was taking a month off to cut cane and was then going to be running an industrial complex for five years.

The newspapers had taken Che's absence from the public eye to mean that Castro and Che had quarreled, or even that Castro had had him shot. One rumor went so far as to say that he had gone insane and had been locked up. Hearing these rumors, Celia was obviously very worried for him and suggested that, if he had fallen out with Castro, perhaps he should go and help one of his friends in Africa. Nonetheless, he was unwilling to change his plans and did not see her.

She died in a clinic in Buenos Aires on May 18, 1965, and was buried in the de la Serna family plot at the Recoleta Cemetery in the city. Her funeral was attended by many of the more prominent members of the Argentine political left and Che's old friend, Ricardo Rojo delivered a eulogy. Her coffin, carried by her husband and two of her sons, was covered with the flags of both Argentina and Cuba, and a small wreath was sent on behalf of Che. Fearful of demonstrations by right wing elements, there was a large police presence.

Che found out at his camp in the Congo via a letter from Castro that was delivered on May 22. He had already suspected she was dying but was very upset when he read the news. He wrote a short story titled "The Stone" in memory of his mother in which he expressed his sense of loss, writing of:

> … *a physical need for my mother to be here so that I can rest my head in her bony lap. I need to hear her call me her "dear old fella" with such tenderness, to feel her clumsy hand in my hair, caressing me in strokes, like a rag doll, the tenderness streaming from her eyes and voice, the broken channels no longer bearing it to the extremities. Her hands tremble and touch rather than caress, but the tenderness still flows from them. I feel so good, so small, so strong. There is no need to ask her for forgiveness. She understands everything. This is evident in her words "my dear old fella"* …

THE WAITING GAME

In the jungle camp, Che tried to improve the education of his men, teaching French, Spanish, and mathematics for a few hours every day. He was himself also trying to learn Swahili in his free time. In this way, he managed to fill the men's time and prevented them from just doing nothing as they waited. The lessons also bound them together and helped create an *esprit de corps*.

He listened to the radio news in the morning, picking up francophone stations and a few in English. French was better, however, as he had never quite got to grips with the English language. He walked every day and used his medical skills when one of the men had a problem. His first letter from the jungle to Aleida explained his routine and expressed his love for her and his children:

To my only one in the world,

(I've borrowed this phrase from old Hickmet)

What miracles you have performed with my poor old shell. I no longer want a real hug and I dream of the concave space in which you comfort me, your smell and your rough rural caresses.

This is another Sierra Maestra, but without the same sense of constructing something or the satisfaction of making it my own. Everything happens very slowly here, as if war was something to be done the day after next. For now, your fear of me being killed is as unfounded as your feelings of jealousy.

My work involves teaching several classes of French every day, learning Swahili and providing medical care. Within a few days I will begin the serious work of training. A sort of Minas del Frio from the war, not the one we visited together.

Give a tender kiss to each child (including Hildita). Take a photo with all of them and send it to me. Not too big and another little one. Study French in preference to nursing and love me.

A long kiss, like our kiss when we are reunited.

I love you,

Tatu

"Tatu" was Swahili for three, and was the name Che used while he was in the Congo.

Che Guevara (left) in the Congo with his troop of Afro-Cuban and Congolese guerrilla fighters, 1965.

THE LONG ROAD AHEAD

Aleida seems to have been pressing to visit him in the Congo. He wrote to her asking her not to blackmail him and reminding her of the kind of man she fell in love with and married:

> Don't try to blackmail me. You can't come now or in three months' time. Maybe in a year it will be different and then we'll see. This has to be properly analyzed. The most important thing is that when you come you aren't "the little wife" but rather a combatant. You must be prepared for that, at least in French …
>
> A good part of my life has been like that: having to hold back the love I feel for other considerations. That's why I might be regarded as a mechanical monster. Help me now Aleida, be strong, and don't create problems that can't be resolved. When we married, you knew who I was. You must do your part so that the road is easier; there is still a long road ahead.
>
> Love me passionately, but with understanding; my path is laid out and nothing but death will stop me. Don't feel sad for me; grab hold of life and make the best of it. Some journeys we will be able to take together. What drives me has nothing to do with a casual thirst for adventure and what that entails. I know that, and so should you.
>
> Educate the children. Don't spoil them or pamper them too much, especially Camilo. Don't think of abandoning them because it isn't fair. They are part of us.
>
> I give you a long and sweet embrace,
>
> Your Tatu

He never stopped asking her to send him books, long lists of classics, everything from Sophocles to Shakespeare.

REMAINING INCOGNITO

Che had moved into the Congo with thirteen Afro-Cubans on April 24, 1965, and things did not go well. There were communication difficulties from the start. Not everyone spoke French and, in fact, not everyone even spoke Swahili, which was the African language that Tanzanians spoke.

Accompanying the group was Godefroi Tchamalesco who, although the most senior Congolese rebel in Dar es Salaam at the time, had no idea who Che was. Remaining incognito suited Che as he was able to get close to the men without them knowing his identity.

In this way, he began to see the dissent in the ranks and was horrified by the lack of discipline. It was very different from the well-drilled and disciplined troops with whom he had fought in the Sierra Maestra. Eventually he had to let Tchamalesco know who he was. Shocked, Tchamalesco left immediately for Cairo to let his boss Laurent Kabila, head of the Congolese rebels, know who they had in their ranks.

Eighteen more Cubans arrived on May 8, accompanied by Kabila's chief of staff, Leonard Mitoudi, who passed on a message from Kabila that Che should continue to keep his identity secret. They moved camp into the mountains at Luluabourg, 3 miles away. Che got on well with Mitoudi but the Congolese chief of staff tragically died while crossing Lake Tanganyika. His death was something of a mystery, but it left Che and his fellow Cuban revolutionaries isolated.

FACING UP TO "MAD MIKE"

Orders were received on June 17 from Kabila to launch an attack on Moïse Tshombe's forces at Fort Bendera which protected a hydroelectric plant on the Kimbi river. The commander of the fort they were facing up to was "Mad Mike" Hoare. The experienced British-Irish mercenary leader had around 100 Belgian paratroopers and 200 African soldiers under his command.

Totally outnumbered, Che was against the idea from the start but the officers of the PLA insisted the attack went ahead. It was a disaster. The soldiers of the Tutsi tribe fled without firing a shot and four Cubans lost their lives. Their identity papers were found by the enemy and it became public knowledge that there were Cubans involved with the PLA.

What made things worse was that by this time the Cuban trainers had still not been able to teach the Congolese how to take aim and fire. They basically just closed their eyes and hoped for the best or fired their bullets into the air. It was a dispiriting business.

EATING YOUR ENEMY'S HEART

It did not help that the Congolese fighters practiced black magic to protect themselves in battle. They believed that a magic potion called Dawa administered by a witch doctor made them invincible. The Africans often boosted their courage under the influence of a variety of other illicit substances as well when they went into battle.

When they realized the magic was failing, they turned on the witch doctor and killed him. Any enemy fighters captured were tortured, and it is thought that the Congolese also indulged in cannibalism, believing that if you ate an enemy's heart you assumed his strength.

Algeria had been the principal supplier of weapons and ammunition to the Congo rebels, so it was a major blow when Ahmed Ben Bella, the Algerian president and Che's great friend, was overthrown in a coup on June 19. The rebel leader Laurent Kabila did finally grace the camp with his presence, turning up in early July. But he quickly had to return to Dar es Salaam to fix other more pressing problems.

NEEDLESS EXTRAVAGANCES

It was deeply frustrating for Che who was well aware that unless the local leaders were present, the indiscipline and lack of focus of the Congolese soldiers was likely to continue. He was disdainful of the leaders of the guerrilla force who took all the perks and privileges they could get, and constantly squabbled over tobacco, alcohol, and other needless extravagances, namely the local prostitutes.

He was completely disgusted too at the sight of Kabila flaunting his high-power status in front of his men when he pulled up at the jungle camp in a Mercedes Benz. But Che's patience was suffering in other ways too—malaria and asthma were both taking their toll on him.

RUMORS FLYING

Meanwhile, back in Cuba, Che's poignant farewell letter was read out by Castro during a public meeting of the newly formed Cuban Communist Party on October 3, 1965. He did it to counteract the rumors flying around about the missing comandante.

Che was disappointed, listening to the speech on the radio in the Congo. He knew that the men he was leading would be very unhappy to hear that in his letter to the Cuban leader he had renounced his Cuban citizenship.

Che also knew that the Cubans had been misled by Gaston Soumialot who had recently visited Havana and given a rosy picture of the situation in the Congo jungle. He explained his fears in a letter to Castro on October 5, saying that he was:

> … worried that, either because I have failed to write with sufficient seriousness or because you do not fully understand me, I may be thought to be suffering from the terrible disease of groundless pessimism … I will just say to you that, according to people close to me here, I have lost my reputation for objectivity by maintaining a groundless optimism in the face of the actual situation. I can assure you that were it not for me this fine dream would have collapsed with catastrophe all around. In my previous letters, I asked to be sent not many people but cadres; there is no real lack of arms here (except for special weapons)—indeed there are too many armed men; what is lacking are soldiers. I especially warned no more money should be given out …

SURROUNDED AT BARAKA

By this time, Che's force and the Congolese PLA were under attack by "Mad Mike" and his mercenaries. They found themselves surrounded at Baraka and soon had to fall back to the nearby town of Fizi. As the mercenaries threatened to advance even further, Che and his men retreated to Luluabourg.

Suddenly, however, President Kasavubu announced that as he believed the rebellion to be virtually defeated, the mercenaries would be leaving the Congo. This resulted in Tanzania and other states that had been supporting the PLA withdrawing their finances.

Che led his men back across the border to Tanzania and before the end of November, Kasavubu had been ousted by Mobutu Sese Soko, as Colonel Mobutu was now calling himself. Mobutu remained in power in the region for more than thirty years.

PRECIOUS LESSONS OF DEFEAT

In the diaries he kept of the Congo campaign, Che's last words are: "I have learned in the Congo, there are mistakes I will never make again, others might be repeated and new ones made." But still he believed in the armed struggle as the only way to achieve what was necessary. "I leave with more faith than ever in guerrilla warfare, but we have failed. My responsibility is great; I will never forget the defeat nor its precious lessons."

One of the fundamental mistakes he made was not ensuring that there was a supreme commander of the force. His disguise at the beginning of the campaign confused the

Crossing Lake Tanganyika from the Congo to Tanzania during the withdrawal of his forces, Che contemplates the failed Congo campaign, 1965.

Congolese but they also could not understand why "Tatu"—number three—was giving orders when he was just the doctor. More important, however, was the fact that the whole country was not willing to fight. A revolution cannot be won by a population unwilling to make sacrifices.

A PARASITICAL ARMY

Che's men returned home after the failure of the Congo campaign while Che remained in Dar es Salaam in December and January, staying out of sight in a small apartment in the grounds of the Cuban embassy.

During this time, he put down on paper his account of the operation in which he is unfailingly honest, even about his own mistakes and misjudgements. He was particularly scathing, however, about Laurent Kabila and his army, describing the PLA as:

> ... a parasitical army, it did not train, it did not fight and it demanded labor and provisions from the locals.

LAST PUBLIC APPEARANCE

Finally Aleida got to spend some time with Che. Castro sent her over to Tanzania while Che was ensconced in the grounds of the embassy. It was one of the few times they were alone together, having always been surrounded by bodyguards or their children.

She spent her time learning French while he developed photographs. He even recorded a few children's stories on tape for her to take back home with her. At that point, he looked different from his familiar image, having only a moustache instead of the ever-present beard.

It all came to an end too quickly and in early 1966 he flew to Prague. Aleida joined him there, traveling as Josefina González and wearing a long black wig and glasses. They spent several weeks in Prague before he planned to head for Bolivia, the venue for his next attempt at revolution.

The ground was already being prepared by Tamara Bunke Bider and his old friend José María Martínez-Tamayo. But Castro wrote him a reminder, suggesting it would not be sensible to go to Bolivia directly from Prague and that he should return to Havana first to plan his campaign more carefully. He reminded him of the facilities that Cuba could offer for the training and selection of the men to accompany him. Che knew only too well that Castro was right.

Therefore, on July 26, with everyone focused on the celebrations for the anniversary of the start of the Cuban Revolution, Che quietly arrived at Havana airport in full disguise, head shaved, wearing glasses, and with a hunched back. He was caught on film that day by a film-maker shooting the arrival of various celebrities for the celebrations, but these scenes were later deleted from the film. It was the last time Che was seen in public.

TIME TO GO

Potential rebels were already in a Cuban training camp at San Andres de Caiguanabo in Pinar del Río province. Aleida accompanied him to the camp and actually trained with the men so she could be with him. The group traveling to Bolivia with him were hardened veterans who Che knew well. They had served with him in the Sierra Maestra and a number had also worked with him after victory. They were a tough, experienced bunch of men who were used to the life of a guerrilla, living rough in the worst terrain.

Finally, it was time to go and Che was taken to a safe house in Havana to see his wife and children for the last time. He was still in disguise and his children were simply told that he was a friend of their father. It must have been a very strange visit indeed, and especially difficult for Aleida who had no idea if she would ever see her husband again.

CHAPTER 16

BOLIVIA: THE LAST CAMPAIGN

THE ÑANCAHUAZÚ GUERRILLAS

Traveling via East Germany and Prague, Che arrived in La Paz, capital of Bolivia, in November 1966. He was posing as a Uruguayan official, Adolfo Mena-González, purportedly in Bolivia on behalf of the Organization of American States to write a report on social and economic conditions in rural Bolivia.

He checked into the Hotel Copacabana before meeting up with three of his men—Harry Villegas-Tamayo (*nom de guerre* Pombo), Alberto de Oca (*nom de guerre* Pacho), and Carlos Coello (*nom de guerre* Tuma) on the evening of November 5. They were driven for two days to an isolated farm in Ñancahuazú where they were to establish their base.

Apparently, the driver of the car who had Che sitting next to him crashed the vehicle into a ditch when he was told who was in the passenger seat and the party had to complete the last 12 miles of their journey on foot. There, others from the Bolivian Communist Party joined them.

The days passed and they did their best to stay out of sight of any neighbors, digging a tunnel to hide their equipment. More men arrived, along with weapons. By the end of November, half the group had arrived and Che reckoned they could remain where they were for a while yet. They needed to try to recruit twenty Bolivians, he noted in his diary.

A clean-shaven Che traveling incognito as Uruguayan official Adolfo Mena-González, 1966.

STAY OR GO—YOU DECIDE

In December, now with a full complement, they worked hard to carve a cave out of a rock in which they could put their radio equipment and another cave was carved out to hide their weapons and food. There was a problem on the last day of December when "Tania" arrived with Mario Monje-Molina (*nom de guerre* Estanislao), Secretary-General of the Communist Party of Bolivia.

Monje demanded that as long as the insurrection was taking place in Bolivia, he should be leader of the group. Monje had never taken part in any kind of guerrilla warfare, and Che was immediately reminded of the confused leadership situation in the Congo. Che insisted that he was in charge and that was the way it would stay.

The two argued and the men in the group from the Bolivian Communist Party were given a choice to go with Monje or stay at the camp. Everyone decided to remain with Che. Monje was furious and withdrew his support.

NO MOOD FOR COMPROMISE

It was a difficult moment because without the support of the Communist Party, the urban network that a revolution needed would be non-existent. But at this stage, Che was in no mood for compromise.

Monje left the next morning, but when asked later why he had challenged a man like Che for the leadership of the insurrection, he said that it was because he was certain that the Bolivian Indians would never follow him. He also insisted that he had been misled; that he had been told that Bolivia was to be merely the jumping-off point for a revolution in Argentina or Peru.

They began to undergo the rigors of training for guerrilla warfare with long, difficult marches. Two men drowned in rivers in February and March, and some of the men, even the veteran Cubans found it tough. A few deserted, a couple were sent home, and one man became an informer to the Bolivian

Army. Equipment was lost too. Hunger and thirst became issues, Che wrote in his diary:

The men are getting increasingly discouraged at seeing the approaching end of the provisions.

NO HIDING PLACE

By March 9, 1967, there were just two meals left and the terrain they were covering was more difficult than any they had so far encountered. For two weeks they had been looking for the Ñancahuazú River to find their way back to the camp but without success.

Finally, they came across Ñancahuazú, almost by accident. They ate their last meal and one of their number was sent to fetch food. Che was relentless throughout their travails.

On March 19, after a particularly tough day when a Bolivian rebel drowned on a training march, Pombo wrote in his diary:

The truth is that I only managed to make it in the first place because the example of Ramón [Che], sick but still among the first, greatly impressed me.

Meanwhile, the sound of a plane's engine constantly droned above them. A Bolivian Army plane had discovered their hiding place.

BOLIVIAN LIBERATION MOVEMENT

On March 20, when they returned from a day's training, they were welcomed by Tania who had brought Ciro Bustos, a man called Chino, and the French intellectual and writer Régis Debray to the camp. Debray spoke fluent Spanish, had worked at Havana University, and had written an influential book about guerrilla warfare. Castro had suggested that he pay the guerrillas a visit in Bolivia. But Che was less impressed, even claiming that when Debray had been captured by the Bolivian Army, he had informed on them.

Debray talked with Che and a few of the men but Che told him the cause would be best served if he went back to France and rallied support. Che gave him letters he had written

REGIS DEBRAY

Born in Paris in 1940, Régis Debray is a French philosopher, journalist, and former French government official. He studied at L'Ecole Normale Superieure where he was taught by Marxist philosopher, Louis Althusser (1918 – 90). During the 1960s, he taught at the University of Havana and later associated with Che in Bolivia.

Debray's 1967 book, *Revolution in the Revolution?* looked at the doctrines espoused by militant socialist movements in Latin America and, as a handbook for guerrilla warfare, supplanted Che's work *Guerrilla Warfare*. He was captured in Bolivia in 1967, and charged with being a member of Che's rebel faction. He was sentenced to thirty years' imprisonment but was released in 1970 after an international campaign to secure his freedom featuring such notable people as Jean-Paul Sartre, André Malraux, Charles de Gaulle, and Pope Paul VI.

On his release, Debray fled to Chile where he wrote *The Chilean Revolution* containing extensive interviews with socialist President Salvador Allende. When Allende was overthrown in 1973, he finally returned to France.

In 1981, when François Mitterand, leader of the Socialist Party, was elected President of France, Debray was appointed as an official advisor to the President on Foreign Affairs. Debray fashioned a policy designed to diminish France's dependence on the United States and promoting good relations with France's former colonies. He resigned in 1988 and went on to occupy a number of other official positions in France.

to Jean-Paul Sartre and Bertrand Russell in which he asked that they establish a fund to provide financial support for the Bolivian Liberation Movement.

He also asked for medicine, electronic equipment, and an electrical engineer. He told Bustos that he should become the movement's representative in Argentina, and gave him letters, one of which was addressed to his father.

PRECISE AND SPECTACULAR

The days continued as before. Messages from La Paz were decoded, some men went out hunting for food, and the men left behind in the camp argued with each other. The Cubans and the Bolivians did not get on. Finally, however, they saw some action.

Early on the morning of March 23, they ambushed a Bolivian Army patrol, consisting of thirty-two men, in the Cañadón de Ñancahuazú, killing seven and taking eleven prisoners. It was a great victory for the guerrillas, especially as they also captured their ammunition, weapons, and radio sets. Best of all, they found the Bolivian Army's operational plan for dealing with them.

"Precise and spectacular" was how Che described the incident in his diary. The story

of the victory was flashed around the world which lifted the rebel spirits after the rigors and tensions of the past weeks.

Not long after, however, Che began to realize that the attack had probably been a mistake. It was as good as lighting a beacon to tell the Bolivian Army there was a team of guerrillas operating in the jungle.

They certainly were not ready for an all-out war. They were all sick, and the quarreling persisted. The central message of Che's *Guerrilla Warfare* books had always been that to stage a successful revolution, the local population's committed support was integral to the rebellion. They had to be carried along the road to revolution by the dynamic zeal of the rebel force. They were nowhere near doing that with the local Bolivians.

GHOSTLY APPARITIONS

Furthermore, their urban network was a mess, with the Communists wanting nothing to do with them. All Che had, in fact, was his band of fighters and they were almost all foreigners.

Others such as Régis Debray, a great admirer of Che, insist that they had little choice but to launch the attack. The authorities had already discovered their whereabouts and there was bound to be an attack on them soon. So Che

In the Bolivian forest, 1967.

was right to go on the offensive, or as one commentator has described it, the "strategic defensive."

Some say the Bolivian Army did not know for sure where the guerrillas were or even if they were a group of organized guerrillas. They certainly did not know that Che was one of them. Bolivian President René Barrientos thought he was dead already as he intimated when asked if Che was responsible:

> *I do not believe in apparitions. I am convinced that he is in the other world with Camilo Cienfuegos and other victims of the Castro regime.*

THE PRESENCE OF GUEVARA

The Bolivians might have been alerted to Che's presence by deserters. Three men had deserted in the first few weeks of March, and Che feared that they had informed on him. Régis Debray agreed when interviewed in his prison cell by a correspondent of Agence France-Presse in November 1967. He was in no doubt that:

> *The presence of Guevara in Ñancahuazú was known by the Army since the beginning of March. It had obtained this information from various sources, principally from the lips of the three deserters who gave three concordant statements.*

It seems, however, that it was probably Tania who inadvertently alerted the Bolivian Army to the presence of the famous Argentinean. When she came back from Argentina, on February 28, she made contact with Bustos and Debray in La Paz. On March 1, she and Bustos boarded a bus to begin their journey to the guerrilla encampment.

AN INVALUABLE DISCOVERY

After several days and using different modes of transport, they hired a jeep that was left in a place called Camiri ready for their return a few days later. But the jeep had been identified by the Bolivian Army as being used

to supply the guerrillas.

The jeep was supposedly "locked away" but the authorities found it along with a sheaf of documents that Tania had left behind. Among these were four notebooks containing the names and addresses of people in Che's urban network and foreign Communist contacts, plus a list of funds and their sources. As a result, many of the members of the urban network were quickly rounded up

This invaluable discovery alerted the authorities to the whereabouts of the camp, leading to the entire region being flooded with soldiers. Leaving the documents in the jeep was a mistake of untold proportions and need not have happened at all since Che had told Tania to return to La Paz immediately and not to go to the camp.

NO WAY BACK FOR TANIA

The often repeated rumor is that Tania disobeyed Che to fulfil her orders from Russia or East Germany to stay close and find out exactly what the plans were. Che was furious when he learned what had happened and Tania broke down in tears when he confronted her, as Bustos later wrote:

> *Ramon seemed ready to vent all his anger and he started in on Tania who left in tears (she had no business in coming; her insubordination had left the guerrilla unit without any contact.)*

Tania had been the link between Che and his urban support network in La Paz and now there was no way back. Her cover was blown.

SUSPICIOUS MINDS

The Army had another lucky break, however, in finding the camp and again it arrived through a piece of insubordination. Another of Che's men—Marcos—had been leading the guerrillas back from yet another training exercise on March 6, when he stopped at an oil-pumping station that was being built by the Bolivian state petroleum corporation.

He was careless and allowed the workers to catch sight of the men's weapons as he tried to buy food which was, in itself, a suspicious thing to do. He claimed to be a Mexican engineer which also aroused suspicious minds. One of the workers, Epifanio Vargas, followed the column of men all the way to their camp at Ñancahuazú.

Once he had seen what he needed, Vargas hurried to the Army's Fourth Division HQ at Camiri with his news. The Army raided the farm at Ñancahuazú. Vargas died in the ambush on March 23 while leading the Army to the camp.

Che had shot men for less back in the Sierra Maestra but for some reason, in this case he chose not to. He simply demoted Marcos, depriving him of his responsibilities and put another man, Miguel, into his place as third in command.

CASTRO-COMMUNISTS

The Army and the Bolivian government were understandably furious about the March 23 ambush. President Barrientos denounced it as being an invasion by:

> *... anarchists from without and within, using foreign slogans, money, and arms and irregular units of diverse origin, especially Castro-communists ...*

It brought Bolivia together in a way that had not happened in years, and political enemies buried the hatchet to condemn the guerrillas. Even the Marxist Party of the Revolutionary Left denounced the ambush as "a violation of the national sovereignty and social and economic progress of the country." Peasant organizations rallied to the government's side and some even took up arms to learn how to combat a guerrilla threat.

Bolivian President René Barrientos denouncing the invading Communist guerrillas to newsmen at a press conference, March 1967.

Still, however, not much was known about the guerrillas and estimates of how many were out there varied greatly. The head of the Bolivian Air Force numbered them at four hundred while some said that the south-eastern region of Bolivia was all but overrun with guerrillas.

Immediately after the ambush, 600 Bolivian soldiers were airlifted into the area but they were hopelessly unprepared for terrain they did not know and found no trace of the guerrillas. The camp was finally discovered on March 31, eight days after the ambush, but Che and his men were long gone.

BOLIVIAN ARMY OF NATIONAL LIBERATION

The Bolivian Army was in a mess, but so were the guerrillas. There was tension still within the group and even dissent. Che berated the men for their training march and how they conducted themselves during the ambush. He was pleased with several of the Cubans who had handled themselves well, in his opinion, but he did not single out any of the Bolivians for praise.

He criticized Marcos for "his despotic attitude toward his comrades" and then threatened four men that if they did not do some work they would not eat. He accused them of not wanting weapons, not helping to carry loads, of feigning illness and one he accused of being a "thief, liar, hypocrite." He described them as the "dregs."

Tension mounted in the days following the action, with thefts of tinned goods and people arguing with one another, disagreeing with comments that were being made. In the middle of all this, Che announced that they now had a new name—Ejército de Liberación Nacional de Bolivia (ELNB), which translates as the Bolivian Army of National Liberation.

By this time, they numbered forty-eight, including Che. Of those, five, including Tania, Bustos, and Régis Debray, were visitors and four were the men he called the "dregs," leaving him with thirty-nine decent fighters. Of these, just twenty-three were Bolivian, while seventeen were Cuban, and three were Peruvian. Nonetheless, Che carried on as if he was somehow representing the entire Bolivian people, issuing "Communiqué No. 1" in their name and a "Manifesto from the Army of National Liberation of the Bolivian People."

THE REAL SIGNIFICANCE

With so few fighting men, it is a miracle that Che gave the Bolivian Army such a hard time during the spring and summer of 1967. Within a seventy-five-mile corridor, they hit the Bolivian Army time and time again. Their best moment was on July 6, when they captured the town of Samaipata and blockaded an important highway between Cochabamba and Santa Cruz.

It was a low-point for the Bolivian Army, government, and people. The country at that time was also beset by a miners' strike that had descended into violence and a wave of popular discontent. It seemed that the Barrientos government would fall at any moment, but it held on grimly to power.

The taking of Samaipata sent a powerful message. The rebels had simply intended to steal a truck and get some medicines and supplies. The place had no industry and little else going for it. But Che recognized the publicity value of commandeering a whole town. Dramatic news bulletins convinced people across the globe that the guerrilla force was much stronger than it really was.

The headlines became even more sensational when the mayor and police chief claimed that Che had been among the guerrillas. His presence was indeed starting to be acknowledged and was formally confirmed when General Alfredo Ovando announced in La Paz on June 30:

> *I wish to announce to the citizenry that the man commanding the guerrillas is the famous Guevara. This may give an idea of the real significance of Ñancahuazú.*

THE TERRIBLE TREK

The strain on the rebels up to this point had been intense and Che, under particular emotional stress, was not in good physical shape through the summer. Moreover, they were eternally hungry. On May 9, an entry in his diary reads:

I felt faint and had to sleep for two hours before I could continue at a slow and vacillating pace. In general, this was the tenor of the whole march. We ate lard soup at the first waterhole. The men are weak and some are suffering from oedema.

Meanwhile, they wandered aimlessly and there were constant thefts from the food store. Che gathered them together one day and went into uncomfortable details:

I criticized Benigno for having eaten a can of food and then denying it; Urbano for having eaten a charqui [dried beef] on the sly; and Aniceto for his eagerness to eat his share of the food, but for not being willing to do his share in other matters.

Then on May 15, Che became seriously unwell:

When we started on the march I was ill with the most violent colic, vomiting, and diarrhea. They stopped it with the demerol, and I lost consciousness while they carried me in a hammock. When I awoke I was much relieved but dirtied all over like a nursing baby. They lent me a pair of pants, but without water my stench extended for a league.

A TRULY LOYAL COMRADE

By the end of June 1967, Che was so ill he could no longer keep up with the rest and was forced to resort to the back of a mule to get around. He was suffering serious asthma attacks and with little medicine left, he had to resort to improvising medicines. On August 2 his last supplies ran out. On August 7, he recorded:

Of the first six men, two are dead, one has disappeared, two are wounded and I with a case of asthma which I am unable to control.

The two dead men were Rolando and Tuma. Rolando, an old companion of Che, had been shot by the Army on April 25, and Tuma had been killed on June 26 in an ambush. Che had taken Rolando's death particularly badly saying:

With his death I lost an irreplaceable, truly loyal comrade of many years standing, and I miss him as I would a son.

Che with his mule Chico in Bolivia, September 1967.

CHAPTER 17

THE BEGINNING OF THE END

On April 17, 1967, Che made one of the biggest mistakes of the campaign. He unaccountably split the group up, ordering Joaquín to "remain around the area" with about a third of the entire force, while he headed with the rest of the group to Muyupampa. They never met up again, and spent the next four months looking for each other.

The Bolivian Army reacted quickly to the taking of Samaipata and launched "Operación Cynthia" to seek and destroy the guerrillas once and for all, followed in early August by "Operación Parabanó." They fought in small units matching the speed and mobility of the guerrillas, and were exceedingly persistent and determined. They did not retreat after a skirmish, they took their losses and pushed on. Relentlessly intent on overwhelming the guerillas, it proved to be the beginning of the end for Che in Bolivia.

DAWN RAID

Joaquín was doggedly tracked by the Fourth Division of the Bolivian Army from the start of Operación Cynthia. The odd clash occurred but nothing serious happened until August 31. He suffered from desertions by Marcos and Victor, and a "visitor," Serapio, was killed. An attack on the road to Taperillas persuaded Chingolo and Eusebio to desert and become informers.

The end for Joaquín's band came at Vado del Yeso just north of the Río Grande. Two undercover soldiers posing as peasants led the Army straight to Joaquín's hideout on a dawn raid.

The guerrillas were at a house trying to buy a calf to kill for food. At about 5:20 that afternoon, as they were making their way across the Masicurí river, holding their guns above their heads to keep them dry, Captain Mario Vargas of the Bolivian Army ordered his men to open fire.

Joaquín and his band stood no chance. One of the first to fall was Tania. Of the ten rebels, only two escaped—Paco and the Peruvian, Médico Negro. The Peruvian was killed later while Paco was taken prisoner and turned informer.

Che heard the news on the *Voice of America* radio show two days later, but refused to believe it, especially as none of the local stations carried the story. The next day, however, when Paco's real name, Jose Carillo, came up on the news, he knew then the Bolivian Army would never give up until the war was won.

TOTALLY CUT OFF

Che and his men were in the inhospitable Province of Vallegrande. Mountainous with no crops, cattle, or game, they lost their way frequently and were hotly pursued by the Bolivian Army. They encountered the fearsome Trinidad Detachment of the Bolivian Army's Eighth Division on July 30, near a place called Moroca. It was a bad day for the guerrillas, as Che admitted in his diary:

My asthma kept me awake all night. At 4:30 as Moro was making coffee he reported seeing a lantern across the river. Miguel ... and Moro went to detain the wanderers. From the kitchen I heard: "Who goes there?" "Trinidad Detachment." Right then the shooting began. Miguel was bringing an M-1 and a cartridge belt from one of the wounded and the news that there were 21 men on the way to Abapó and 150 in Moroca. We caused them more casualties but were unable to determine these because of the confusion that ensued.

The rebels made their retreat with twelve men covering them. Two of these were killed crossing the river and a third was killed bravely trying to rescue them. Another died later. They also lost much of their supplies, as Che noted:

… 11 knapsacks containing medicines, binoculars and equipment such as the tape recorder used for copying the messages from Manila [being the code name for Havana], Debray's book with my notations, a book by Trotsky, not to mention the political significance that the capture of these items has for the government and the confidence that it gives the soldiers.

The loss of the tape recorder was a catastrophe. It was used to record coded messages from Havana that could be decoded later. They were now totally cut off.

UP AHEAD IN THE DISTANCE

When the guerrillas reached La Higuera, a hamlet north-west of Vado del Yeso, it was just about empty. There were a few women left, but all the men had vanished. Che decided they should head for the next town, Jagüey, where apparently a fiesta was taking place. A few of them set off and Che and some others remained to bring up the rear.

While he was talking to the only man left in La Higuera, a coca drug smuggler turned up saying he had been around the area and had seen no evidence of the Army. The men seemed exceptionally nervous. Probably to be expected given the circumstances, Che thought. He suspected both were lying to him but let them go.

Thirty minutes after the first group left, Che and the remaining men set off. It was 1:30 p.m. as he started to climb a hill, but suddenly up ahead in the distance bursts of gunfire rang out:

With the assistance of the local population, Che (seated right) studies a map of the Pesca River region.

CIRO BUSTOS

Argentine artist Ciro Bustos first met Che in his office at the Ministry of Industry. His first impression was that the revolutionary was very matter-of-fact, without the bombast of Fidel Castro and with a sense of humor. The two hit it off immediately and Che selected him to take part in Jorge Masetti's attempt to instigate revolution in Argentina.

In 1967 Che asked Bustos to join him in Bolivia to create a continental revolution in Latin America. As the Bolivian Army closed in on the guerrillas in the jungle, Bustos left the camp but was taken prisoner. For three weeks, he was interrogated, but maintained his innocence. But the CIA and the Bolivian Army were well aware of the identities of the rebels including Che, and Bustos agreed to sketch some of the guerrillas, believing they were probably dead.

Bustos was sentenced to thirty years' imprisonment on the same day Che Guevara was captured. He spent three years in prison but was freed when a leftist general came to power in Bolivia. He traveled to Chile and then returned to Argentina. In 1976 he was forced to seek refuge in Sweden after his life was threatened by right-wing death squads who were murdering dissidents.

Bustos has often been dubbed "the man who betrayed Che Guevara" because of the drawings he made. In his 2007 memoir *Che Wants to See You*, he hoped to vindicate himself, but the soubriquet has always stuck and is forever associated with his name. Ciro Bustos died in Malmo in 2017, he was 85 years old.

… the sound of firing all over the ridge told us that our men [the ones who had left in advance] had fallen into an ambush. I organized the defense … and designated as the retreat route a road which would lead to the Rio Grande.

ROCK-BOTTOM

Miguel, Coco, and Julio died in the ambush, a defeat that brought Che to his lowest point, as if he could see disaster looming ahead. Everything seemed desperate. He wanted to find an escape route but even if they figured a way out, there was no outside network to help them. The contacts in La Paz had all been arrested. "Defeat" was the only word in Che's diary entry for September 26.

He had just seventeen men left and his health was getting worse, affecting his thinking and his decision-making. As his asthma debilitated him even more, he made the decision to send three men to fetch his medicine from where it had been buried at Ñancahuazú. A risky business, to say the least.

He was also taking three men out of his small band which could prove disastrous.

He was not the only one suffering however. They all had malnutrition from eating a diet of snakes and rotten cats. They even slaughtered the horse Che had been riding for the last few months and ate it. The men were collapsing through lack of food and water and enduring dizziness, diarrhea, and stomach cramps. Morale was at rock-bottom.

THE LAST DIARY ENTRY

The rebels had no idea where the enemy was, but they knew the Army were on their heels. The information that the peasants gave them could not be trusted and radio reports were unreliable. The reality was that the Bolivian Fourth Division who had been pursuing Che for seven months, had now set up new headquarters at Padilla, just fifty miles south of La Higuera. Che's survival instincts kept him heading north-west toward Cochabamba and La Paz.

The guerrillas of the Ñancahuazú with Che second from left.

Che may have believed it was the only escape route left open to him as the Army closed in. Things were increasingly desperate and on September 28, he wrote in his diary: "A day of anguish. At times it seemed as if it would be our last." From this point on they were all bad days.

October 7, 1967, marked eleven months since they came together as a guerrilla army. That day Che believed they were about three miles from the village of La Higuera and perhaps six miles from Pucara. In a canyon at Quebrada del Yuro, they detained a woman goat-herder to prevent her informing the Army of their location. When two guerrillas went to the woman's house they found her two daughters.

Traveling under cover of darkness became impossible when the Peruvian, Chino, lost his glasses. He could see nothing without them and his continual stumbling forced them to stop for the night. They bedded down at around 2:00 a.m. on October 8, with water to drink from the streams and wild potatoes to eat. Che wrote in his diary that night that he did not believe any of the radio reports he was hearing. It was his last diary entry.

I AM CHE

A peasant woman—it is not known if she was the same woman the guerrillas detained—alerted the Army that she had heard voices along the banks of the Yuro river. The dogged Bolivian Fourth Division had done all the hard work, tracking Che for seven months. But now that the end was nigh, the CIA-assisted Bolivian Rangers moved in looking to claim the credit for Che's capture.

The Rangers took up positions in the canyon where the guerrillas were sleeping. At midday a unit of soldiers who had recently graduated from a US Army Special Forces training camp opened fire on the guerrillas, killing two of them and wounding others.

Che's last battle began at 1:30 p.m. Willy Sarabia, a Bolivian miner who had joined the guerrillas, was at the front of the rebels and behind him was Che who had received several bullet wounds to his leg. Sarabia tried to pick

Che up and carry him away from the gunfire but a bullet tore off Che's iconic beret.

Sarabia carefully placed Che on the ground so that he could return fire but the Rangers encircled the pair. Che was trying to return fire but had only one good arm and was unable to raise his rifle. Another bullet ripped into his right leg, and he was also hit on the right forearm. His gun was knocked out of his hand. Soldiers began to run toward him and he shouted out:

> Do not shoot!
> I am Che Guevara …
> worth more to you alive than dead.

The battle came to an end at 3:30 p.m.

WE HAVE PAPA

Sarabia and Che both survived and were brought before the Bolivian Rangers Captain, Gary Prado, who ordered his radio operator to send a coded signal to divisional headquarters in Vallegrande to inform them that Che had been captured. The code for this had earlier been agreed to be "Hello Saturno, we have Papá." "Saturno" was Colonel Joaquín Zenteno, commander of the Eighth Bolivian Army Division; "Papá" was the codename for Che.

Zenteno could not believe it, and the message was repeated. When it was confirmed that Che had indeed been taken prisoner, joyous celebrations erupted throughout divisional headquarters. Zenteno replied to Prado that Che and any other captives should be immediately transferred to La Higuera. The message came back from Prado, "Papá cansado," meaning "Papá is tired." Code for "Che is wounded."

Che was put on a blanket and carried by four soldiers the four miles to La Higuera, Willy Sarabia forced to limp along, his hands tied behind his back. It was early evening and getting dark when they arrived in La Higuera. Che and Sarabia were put in the one-room schoolhouse and later that night five more dead or dying guerrillas were brought to La Higuera.

Wounded and defeated, Che is held by Bolivian Rangers after his capture at La Higuera, with CIA agent Félix Rodríguez on the left.

MIXED EMOTIONS

Meanwhile, official army dispatches were falsely claiming that Che had been killed and that the Army had his body. The Bolivian High Command did not confirm or deny these reports.

At 6:15 a.m. on October 9, CIA operative Félix Rodríguez arrived at La Higuera by helicopter accompanied by Colonel Zenteno. Rodríguez had a powerful portable field radio and a camera with a four-foot stand that was used to photograph documents.

Rodríguez later recalled the scene as "gruesome." Che lay bleeding in the dirt in the schoolhouse, his arms tied behind his back and his feet tied together. Beside him lay the dead bodies of his friends.

"A piece of trash" is how Rodríguez described the way he looked. His black hair was long and matted, his clothes were torn, and on his feet he wore two pieces of leather for shoes:

I had mixed emotions when I first arrived there. Here was the man who had assassinated many of my countrymen. And nevertheless, when I saw him, the way he looked … I felt sorry for him.

Rodríguez set up his radio and transmitted a coded message to a CIA station in either Peru or Brazil that was forwarded to CIA headquarters at Langley, Virginia. Rodríguez began using his special camera to photograph Che's diary and other documents that the Bolivian Army had found with the guerrillas. He later talked to Che and took a picture of him.

LET HISTORY TAKE ITS COURSE

By 10:00 a.m. the question was: what were they going to do with the captured guerrilla leader? A trial was considered unworkable. Attention would be focused on it from around the world, possibly eliciting sympathetic propaganda for Che and Cuba. It was decided he should be executed at once. The official story would claim later that Che died from wounds received in battle.

A call came through from HQ at Vallegrande and Rodríguez was ordered to conduct "Operation Five Hundred and Six Hundred." "Five Hundred" was the Bolivian Army's code for Che and "Six Hundred" was the code for him to be killed.

Rodríguez passed the order to Colonel Zenteno but also alerted him that the United States government had instructed him to keep Che alive at all costs. He had helicopters and planes ready to fly Che to Panama for interrogation. Zenteno replied he had to obey the orders of his own commander. Rodríguez realized there was little he could do, deciding, as he later put it, "to let history take its course."

BETTER LIKE THIS

When the order came, Che was asked if he wanted anything before the execution. Che replied that all he wanted was to "die with a full stomach." Asked if he was a materialist, Che answered "perhaps." Meanwhile, Willy Sarabia was being executed in another building.

When one of the school teachers informed Zenteno that she had heard a report on the radio that Che was dead, Zenteno realized that he could no longer delay. He went into the schoolhouse and informed Che of the order from his superiors. Che understood and said:

> It is better like this …
> I never should have been captured alive.

He gave Rodríguez a message each for Aleida and Castro. He and Rodríguez embraced and the American left the room.

THE SHORT STRAW

Straws were drawn among the non-commissioned officers present to determine who was going to carry out the execution. Sergeant Mario Terán drew the short straw and went to the schoolhouse.

He found Che propped up against the wall. Che asked to be allowed to stand up. Terán, frightened by what he had to do, backed out of the room, only to be ordered to return again by the senior officers.

The Bolivian Rangers who were responsible for the capture and execution of Che Guevara on October 8, 1967.

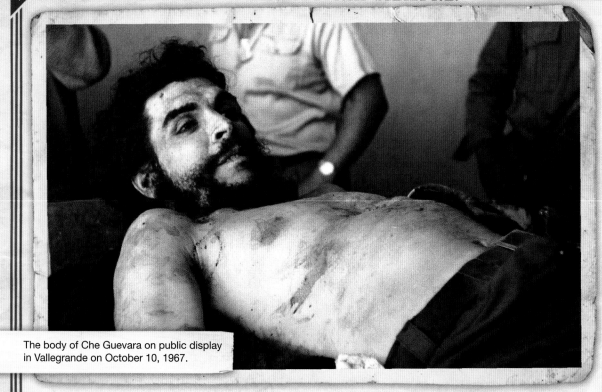

The body of Che Guevara on public display in Vallegrande on October 10, 1967.

Trembling, he returned to the schoolhouse. Averting his eyes from Che's face, he fired into his chest and side. Several other soldiers, wanting to say they shot Che, rushed into the schoolhouse and also fired into his body. It was 1:10 p.m., October 9, 1967.

When Terán entered the schoolhouse and raised his M2 Carbine, he heard the last words that Che would ever speak:

I know you have come to kill me.
Shoot, you are only going to kill a man.

AFTERMATH

Rodríguez left La Higuera in a helicopter along with the other senior Bolivian Army officers later that afternoon. Landing at Vallegrande, he quickly exited the helicopter with a Bolivian Army hat pulled down over his face, knowing Castro's men would be there watching for CIA operatives.

Another helicopter flew Che's body to Vallegrande and the body was fingerprinted and embalmed. Two doctors signed his death certificate on October 10, at the Hospital Knights of Malta in Vallegrande. The certificate stated:

… on October 9 at 5:30 p.m., there arrived … Ernesto Guevara Lynch, approximately 40 years of age, the cause of death being multiple bullet wounds in the thorax and extremities. Preservative was applied to the body.

That same day the autopsy report spoke of multiple bullet wounds to Che's body, but that the cause of death "was the thorax wounds and consequent haemorrhaging."

BURIAL AND REDISCOVERY

At first, his family refused to believe that Che was dead. Che's father was very firmly in denial about it. On October 12, however, Che's brother Roberto Guevara arrived in Vallegrande to take the body back home. He was told a blatant lie by General Ovando that Che's body had already been cremated. Roberto returned home alone.

The reality was that the body had been secretly buried at an isolated airstrip at Vallegrande. Che's hands were amputated after his death so the Argentine police could confirm that the dead man was indeed Che Guevara.

The body was rediscovered in 1997, along with the remains of six other men, by a team of Cuban geologists and Argentine forensic anthropologists. The hands of one of the dead were missing which helped to confirm that it was actually Che.

The remains of all seven were brought back to Cuba in 1997, and laid to rest with military honors in a mausoleum that had been constructed in the Cuban city of Santa Clara, the site of Che's most famous victory during the Cuban Revolution.

LEGENDS WILL BE CREATED

On October 18, 1967, the third day of national mourning for the loss of Che, Castro delivered a eulogy to the fallen guerrilla before a crowd of a million people in the Plaza de la Revolución in Havana. Reaching the high point of his speech toward the end of his tribute, Castro declared his final salutation to Che:

> *If we want to know how we want our children to be, we should say, with all our revolutionary mind and heart: We want them to be like Che.*

A dispatch from Richard Gott, a *Guardian* journalist in Vallegrande on the day of the execution, defined Che perfectly as a man whose powerful presence across the globe, even in time of death, lived on for generations and transformed him into a revolutionary icon:

> *It was difficult to recall that this man had once been one of the great figures of Latin America. It was not just that he was a great guerrilla leader; he had been a friend of presidents as well as revolutionaries.*
>
> *His voice had been heard and appreciated in inter-American councils as well as in the jungle. He was a doctor, an amateur economist, once Minister of Industries in revolutionary Cuba, and Castro's right-hand man. He may well go down in history as the greatest continental figure since Bolivar.*
>
> *Legends will be created around his name.*

Fidel Castro announcing Che's death on the radio.

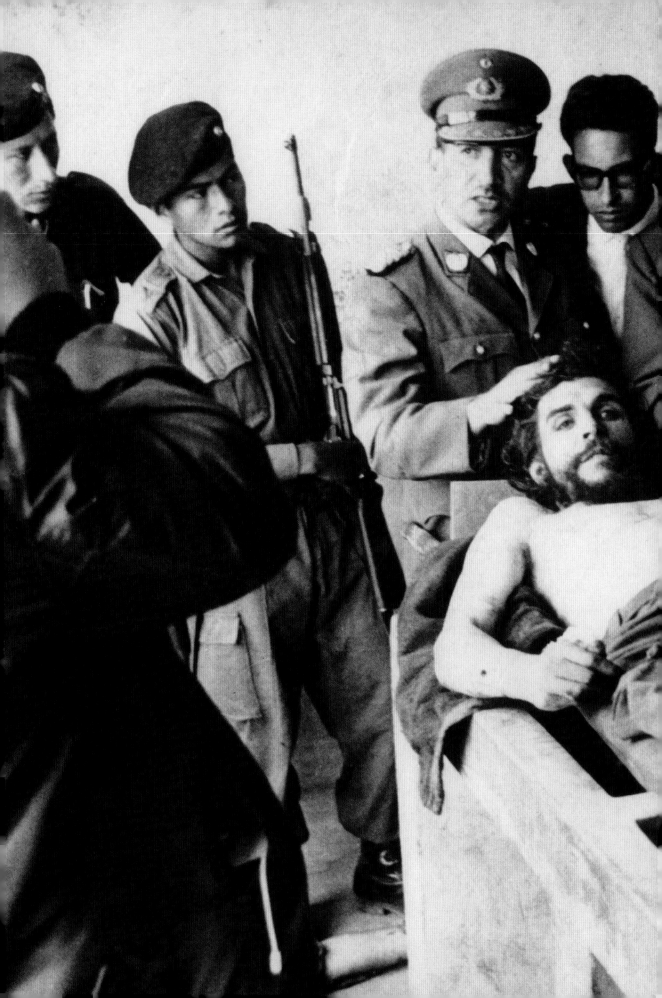

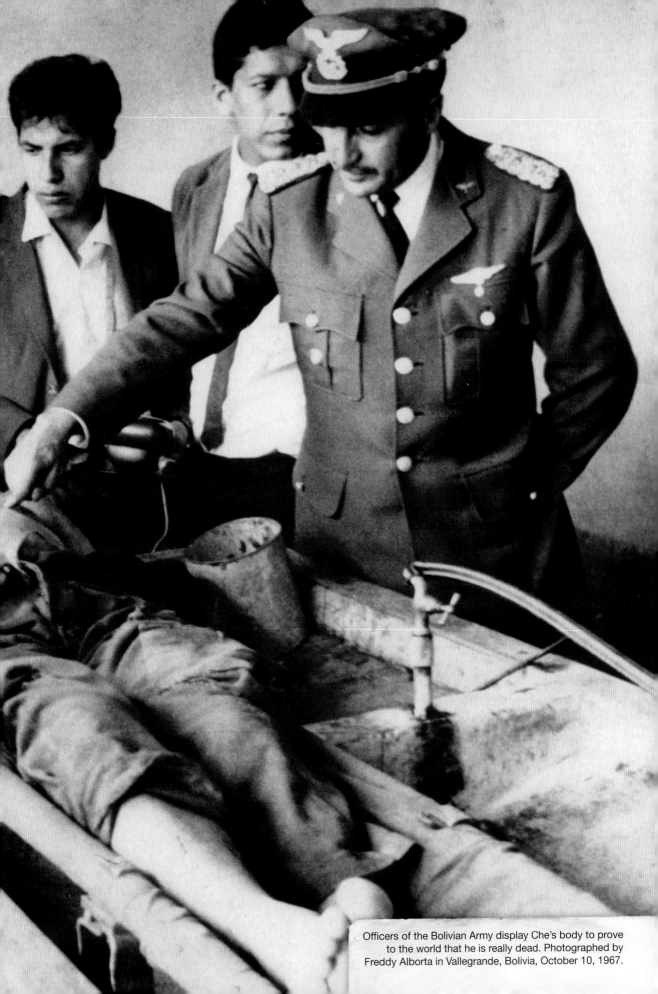

Officers of the Bolivian Army display Che's body to prove to the world that he is really dead. Photographed by Freddy Alborta in Vallegrande, Bolivia, October 10, 1967.

PART FIVE

CHE LIVES FOREVER!

THE TURNING POINT IN EACH MAN'S LIFE IS THE
MOMENT IN WHICH HE DECIDES TO FACE DEATH.

CHE GUEVARA

Cubans are introduced to the legend of Che at an early age. A young boy laughs along with the smiling revolutionary hero during the May Day parade in Plaza de la Revolución, Havana, 2007.

CHAPTER 18

THE INFINITE REVOLUTIONARY

It is not hard to imagine that Che Guevara would be appalled by the image of himself that has grown through the decades since he was executed at La Higuera. He has almost ceased to be a man who lived and breathed and has become an icon, a symbol of the counterculture, or just a decoration for a T-shirt. Ciro Bustos has said that were Che to return and see the famous photograph of him by Alberto Korda adorning T-shirts, he would be horrified and would think he had failed.

A SYMBOL OF REBELLION

In fact, the sanctification and mythologizing of the guerrilla leader began almost immediately after his death. The pictures of his Christ-like dead body flashed around the globe, resulting in protest demonstrations around the world. Songs were sung about him, poems written, and tributes were paid everywhere.

Those of the political left glorified him as a revolutionary who heroically sacrificed himself for the cause of liberty and freedom from oppression. He became a powerful symbol of rebellion during the May 1968 protests and unrest in France. Gary Younge of *The Guardian* noted how:

> [Che's] journey from middle-class comfort to working-class champion and his long-haired unkempt look, mirrored the aspirations and self-image of the Woodstock generation as they demonstrated against the Vietnam war.

The graffiti slogan "Che lives!" began to appear on walls, and people spoke glowingly of him as a human being, ignoring the violence and killing that he perpetrated during his life. The great existentialist, Jean-Paul Sartre, who had visited him in Havana, described him as "the most complete human being of our age."

PATRIA O MUERTE

To Cubans, Che is the epitome of revolutionary values, a national hero who is revered and whose 22-feet-tall statue looks down on the scene of his greatest moment, when his guerrilla force took Santa Clara. That was the moment Fulgencio Batista decided to flee, and the revolution was won.

His adopted country Cuba continues to honor him, not just in the mausoleum complex that holds his and many other Cuban fighters' remains but in schoolrooms, workplaces, public buildings, billboards, and on banknotes. Given Che's attitude toward money, it is unlikely that he would have been pleased.

His famous image can be found on postage stamps and on the 3-peso coin, resplendent with starred beret and flowing locks beneath the words "Patria o Muerte"—My Country or Death.

GUEVARISMO

Guerrilla warfare as a means of achieving its foreign policy objectives was abandoned by the Cuban government after Che's death. The country sent troops to Africa in the 1970s, but it was a proper force that was sent and not a guerrilla group. Revolutionary movements in Latin America were still supported by Cuba but they were more in the background and they never again sent a force of trained guerrillas such as Che's to another country.

In revolutionary movements, there has, however, been a resurgence of the sort of ideas Che was championing. In the 1990s when it was perceived that liberal reforms had failed, antagonism toward the United States increased, and notions such as Pan-Americanism became popular again, as did nationalization of key industries and the centralization of government.

"Guevarismo," as it has been called, has been present, to a greater or lesser extent in many revolutionary movements in Argentina, Chile, Nicaragua, and El Salvador. The Sandinistas in Nicaragua had ideas similar to Che's and when they finally came to power in 2006 after a sixteen-year struggle, supporters celebrated wearing Che Guevara T-shirts.

Bolivian President Evo Morales has paid tribute to Che and has a portrait of him made from coca leaves in his presidential suite. The late Venezuelan President Hugo Chávez often addressed crowds clad in a T-shirt with Che's image on it and described him as an "infinite revolutionary."

The Colombian revolutionaries the FARC (Fuerzas Armadas Revolucionarias de Colombia) are inspired by Che's guerrilla activities, as are the mostly indigenous Mexican Zapatistas based in Chaipas in the south of the country.

THE CULT OF CHE GUEVARA

In September 2007, Che was voted Argentina's greatest historical and political figure, a remarkable achievement, given that he visited the country only once after he left it in 1953. Undoubtedly, however, there is what has been described as a "cult of Che Guevara."

Alberto Korda's photograph of him became one of the images of the twentieth century. Transformed into a monochrome graphic titled "Viva Che" in 1968 by Irish artist Jim Fitzpatrick, it has become an ubiquitous image, found on cigarette packs, posters, coffee mugs, baseball caps, and, of course, T-shirts.

The crass view is of Che as a rock star, the handsome revolutionary, in the words of the British journalist Sean O'Hagan "more Lennon than Lenin." But that is the opinion of someone with little knowledge of Che's thinking and his approach to politics and society. One of Che's biographers, Jorge Castaneda, reminds us that Che's place is "in the niches reserved for cultural icons, for symbols of social uprisings that filter down deep into the soil of society."

Castaneda points out that Che actually did die for what he believed. Still, however, the image of Che has become dissociated from his revolutionary message and many who wear the T-shirts have no idea what the man stood for.

T-shirts with multiple images of Che on display in Havana, Cuba.

Cubans wave photos of Che in the Plaza de la Revolución during the celebrations for the fiftieth anniversary of his death, October 8, 2017.

CHAPTER 19

CHE ON THE PAGE

CHE GUEVARA'S DIARIES

The Motorcycle Diaries has become a cult work both in Latin America and elsewhere in the world, securing a place for Che alongside the road trip adventures of Jack Kerouac. He was a prolific writer and his oeuvre contains writings on Marxism and social theory. He also wrote about his campaigns or kept diaries. A sequel was published—*Latin American Diaries*—covering his second trip in 1953, the one that led him to Guatemala and then Mexico City, Fidel Castro, and his future as a revolutionary warrior.

During his lifetime, he published *Reminiscences of the Cuban Revolutionary War* in which, for the first time, he talks of the *foco* approach to revolution, how a popular force can win against a much larger army without having to wait until the conditions are right; the insurrection itself will create those conditions.

Guerrilla Warfare, his manual of how to conduct a guerrilla war was published once the revolutionaries came to power in Cuba and he produced a sequel in *Guerrilla Warfare: A Method*.

The African Dream was a book that told the story of his brief adventure in the Congo. It opens with the words "This is the story of a failure." In the book he is as critical of himself as he is of the Africans alongside whom he was fighting.

The Bolivian Diary was Che's last book and it benefits from his rigorous diary-keeping. As Fidel Castro said of the book: "Thanks to Che's invariable habit of noting the main events of each day, we have rigorously exact, priceless and detailed information on the heroic final moments of his life in Bolivia." It provides an uncompromising portrait of a highly disciplined, single-minded man.

MEMOIRS & BIOGRAPHIES

WRITTEN BY FRIENDS

It seems almost anyone who came into contact with the charismatic guerrilla leader has felt the need to write a book about him. The title choice therefore is wide-ranging and covers every part of his life, from his childhood through his peregrinations around his continent to his ill-fated Bolivian expedition.

Congolese citizens Floribert Milimba (right) and Tabu Aziza look at a copy of Che Guevara's *The African Dream*, some fifty years after they met him during the failed 1965 campaign to bring revolution to the Congo.

Both his companions on his journeys have put pen to paper, recalling the incidents on the road and the slow awakening of Che's political consciousness. *Traveling with Che Guevara: The Making of a Revolutionary* by Alberto Granado, his fellow traveler on his first journey, is a companion piece to Che's *The Motorcycle Diaries*. Granado gives his side of the story in a moving and hilarious account of how two young men set out to find adventure but ended up finding their true purpose in life, Granado as a scientist and Che as a revolutionary.

Che's second trip in Latin and Central America is told by the man who accompanied him, Carlos "Calica" Ferrer, in *Becoming Che: Guevara's Second and Final Trip through Latin America*. The young Ernesto is depicted as his political awareness grows until he sees a revolution thwarted in Guatemala and meets up with Fidel Castro in Mexico City, committing himself to the Cuban Revolution and, as Ferrer puts it, becoming Che.

Che's friend, the Argentinean Ricardo Rojo, whom he met during his second journey around Latin and Central America in 1953 when Che's political awareness was growing, has written the fascinating *My Friend Che* in which he tells us of their friendship and also talks of the darkest period of Che's life when he was having problems with Fidel Castro in 1965. He also chronicles the dreadful Bolivian struggle.

In 1997, three decades after Che's demise at La Higuera, a number of friends and family including Che's widow, Aleida March, contributed to *Che's Companeros: Witnesses to a Legend*. Contributors recall Che as both a man and a leader and the book is beautifully illustrated by the photographs of internationally renowned photographer, Francis Giacobetti.

WRITTEN BY THE GUEVARA FAMILY
Che's family have written books about him, most notably his father, Ernesto Guevara Lynch. His 2007 book, *Young Che: Memories of Che Guevara by His Father* was assembled from two previous books by him—*My Son Che* and *A Soldier of the Americas*. The narrative takes us through Che's bourgeois but unconventional childhood, detailing the people, events, and books that helped to shape the man he became. It draws on his letters home and includes his diary of his bicycle trip around Northern Argentina in 1950.

Che's brother waited fifty years to share intimate memories of his famous sibling. In *Che, My Brother* Juan Martín Guevara tells of their young lives together as well as the two months he spent with Che in Havana in 1959. Juan Martín also writes about their parents Ernesto and Celia, as well as other members of the eccentric Guevara family.

Che's two wives have shared their memories of him in books. *Ernesto: A Memoir of Che Guevara*, by Che's first wife Hilda Gadea, describes her time with him, shedding light on the development of his political ideas before he met Fidel Castro in Mexico City. Hilda's book was published in 1972, just five years after her husband's death.

Aleida March, his second wife, with whom he had four children, waited forty-one years to share her memories with us. *Remembering Che: My Life with Che Guevara* appeared in 2008 and it describes their great romance from the days when she was a fellow combatant in the Sierra Maestra during the Cuban Revolution up to the terrible moment when she learned of her husband's execution in Bolivia.

WRITTEN BY FELLOW FIGHTERS
A number of the men who fought alongside Che have contributed to our knowledge of the man. Fidel Castro, who perhaps knew him best, provides a vivid and surprisingly moving portrayal of the man, the revolutionary, and the thinker in *Che: A Memoir*. Castro recalls Che's time in Cuba, especially the last days he spent in his adopted country and gives a frank appraisal of Che's last campaign in Bolivia.

Harry Villegas—*nom de guerre* Pombo—was just 17 when he joined Che's column in Castro's force. He later fought with him in the doomed Congo expedition as well as in Bolivia, one of only six Bolivian and Cuban guerrillas to survive. *At the Side of Che Guevara: Interviews with Harry Villegas (Pombo)* is a 36-page pamphlet comprising two interviews with Pombo.

Manuel Piñeiro, or "Barbarroja" (Red Beard) as he was known, was a shadowy figure who oversaw the revolutionary operations in Cuba and Africa when he worked closely with Che. In his book, *Che Guevara and the Latin American Revolution*, he offers some fascinating insights into Che's thinking about revolution in Latin America. Piñeiro eventually emerged from the shadows in 1997, but died in a car crash shortly after.

The Marxist philosopher Régis Debray was present for a short time with Che in the Bolivian jungle in 1967, before being arrested and imprisoned by the Bolivians. In his book, *Che's Guerrilla War*, he analyzes some of the mistakes and miscalculations Che made in that campaign that led to disaster and, ultimately, his death.

Rodolfo Saldaña was a Bolivian member of Che's Bolivian escapade and one of the few survivors. In his book, *Fertile Ground: Che Guevara and Bolivia: A First-hand Account*, the "fertile ground" to which he refers in the title is the plight of Bolivian tin miners, peasants, and indigenous people that made Che's Bolivian Revolution seem possible.

Ciro Bustos, an Argentinean from Mendoza, was recruited into the Cuban spy network in the early 1960s by Che. In *Che Wants to See You: The Untold Story of Che Guevara*, he tells the story of Che's ambitious plan to export revolution to Latin America. Bustos worked with him both in the aborted Argentinean revolution and during the operation in Bolivia.

Victor Dreke, second-in-command in the Congo, was one of Che's right-hand men. In *From the Escambray to the Congo: In the Whirlwind of the Cuban Revolution* (2002), he talks about the Cuban Revolution and what it meant to Cubans, especially in the way that it dismantled the racial discrimination that had been part of Cuban life in the time of Fulgencio Batista's government. Dreke points out that although Che's Congo revolution failed, it laid the foundations for later Cuban efforts to help Africans in their revolutionary struggles.

FICTION AND THRILLERS

As Che's life reads like fiction, and his inspiration continues to this day, it is little surprise that novelists have turned to him.

Teresa De La Caridad Doval uses the inspirational side of Che in her novel *A Girl Like Che Guevara*. This coming-of-age novel tells the story of 16-year-old Lourdes, a dedicated Cuban revolutionary who spends the summer of 1982 working at the "School-in-the-Fields," toiling in the tobacco fields to prove her commitment to Fidel Castro and the Cuban Revolution. She is filled with contradictions and questions, especially the question of why she wants to be like Che.

In *I, Che Guevara: A Novel* John Blackthorn uses Che as the vehicle for a thriller. In the summer of 1999, a mysterious old stranger named Ernesto Blanco appears in Cuba, advocating a new type of politics that he describes as "The True Republic." Older Cubans begin to suspect that the stranger is actually Che Guevara who had not been killed

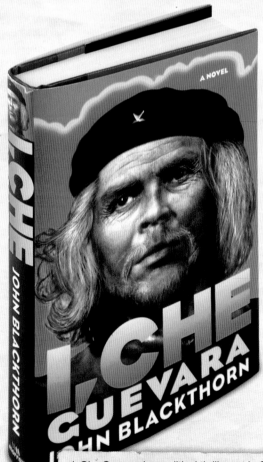

I, Che Guevara is a political thriller set in Cuba written by John Blackthorn, the pseudonym for former US Senator Gary Hart.

in Bolivia after all. When Fidel Castro steps down, two political parties vie for power and as Ernesto Blanco's True Republic movement gains momentum, the two parties plot to kill him.

Staying truer to actual history in *Killing Che*, terrorism expert Chuck Pfarrer has created an intense cat-and-mouse thriller. In the book Che did not die in 1967, but is leading a Cuban-inspired insurgency in Bolivia. World-weary CIA paramilitary officer, Paul Hoyle, draws ever closer to the great guerrilla fighter in the Bolivian jungle.

Another book that is based on the notion that Che did not die is *Operation Che Guevara* written by Nick Carter. In this exciting novel, Number 49 in the "Killmaster Series," the world thinks Che died in that schoolroom in La Higuera, but two beautiful women share a deadly secret and Nick Carter has every reason to believe that the great Cuban revolutionary has been kept alive.

In *See You Later Alligator*, author William F. Buckley Jr. puts his CIA agent Blackford Oakes into action. Oakes is selected by President Kennedy to have a meeting with Che Guevara in Cuba. Kennedy has contrived a plan—Operation Alligator—that he hopes will bring a period of calm to US-Cuban relations. However, the communists have other ideas, with a plot to badly destabilize the region and bring an end to Kennedy's presidency.

Equally fanciful and a lot more explosive is *Special Ops* by W.E.B. Griffin. In the ninth of his hugely successful "Brotherhood of War" series, Griffin pitches a team of Special Forces operatives against Che Guevara with thrilling consequences.

One particularly notable novel about Che is Jay Cantor's *The Death of Che Guevara* published in 2005. In this critically acclaimed first novel, Cantor tells the epic story of Che Guevara's life and death. While following Che's political evolution, it also charts the revolutionary struggles of Latin America and examines what it means to be a revolutionary activist.

ROMANCE

Several novels feature Che as the romantic leading man, somewhat stretching historical credibility.

In *A Kiss for Señor Guevara* by Terence Clarke, the young Ofelia is delegated to care for Che Guevara in La Higuera during the last few days of his life. In their few moments alone, each discovers the possibility of love in the middle of horrific warfare.

Becoming Tania: A Novel of Love, Revolution and Betrayal by Ian Adams invents a love affair between Che and Tamara Bunke Bider—Tania the Guerrilla—in a tale of espionage, love, and betrayal in revolutionary times.

There is more unlikely romance for Che in *Loving Che* by Ana Menèndez. Searching for details of her birth mother, a young Cuban woman uncovers the fact that her mother had an affair in her youth with the handsome and charismatic Che Guevara that resulted in the birth of a child. The novel brilliantly recaptures the excitement, the hopes, the disappointments, and the terror of those revolutionary times.

GRAPHIC NOVELS

Since the 1960s, the graphic novel has established itself as one of the most prominent countercultural art forms and it is ideally suited to telling the story of Che Guevara. There are several fine examples.

Che: A Graphic Biography is a graphic novel by Sid Jacobson and Ernie Colon. This book uses wonderfully vibrant illustrations to tell the story of Che's life and achievements, from his motorcycle journeys with Alberto Granado to his execution in Bolivia.

The late Spain Rodriguez has been described as "one of the true giants of the comics medium" by another master of the art form, Joe Sacco. His *Che: A Graphic Biography* is a powerfully illustrated and extensively researched graphic novel on the life of Che.

The Japanese Manga style has been used to good effect in the telling of Che's life story by Kiyoshi Konno & Chie Shimano in *Che Guevara: A Manga Biography*. It is evident from the book that Konno is a huge fan of Che. His presentation of him is fairly uncritical, but the drawing is powerful and effective and its scathing critique of American foreign policy is particularly potent. Che's exciting life is perfect material for the format.

Che Guevara for Beginners by Sergio Sinay provides the reader with a very basic grounding in the fascinating story of Che Guevara's life and may encourage him or her to move on to a more comprehensive telling of the great revolutionary's life and achievements.

The Last Days of Che Guevara: A Graphic Novel by Marco Rizzo and Lelio Bonaccorso is an illustrated retelling of Che's final hours in La Higuera. It starts at the point at which the wounded Che was captured by the Bolivian Army in October 1967 and depicts his murder and the global reaction to it.

The renowned comic-book artwork of Spain Rodriguez is a powerful feature in *Che: A Graphic Biography*.

PHOTOGRAPHIC BOOKS

Naturally, this most photogenic man is bound to have engendered a number of books showing him in all his handsome glory. Several of the photographic books about Che focus on that most fascinating of all photos, Alberto Korda's *Guerrillero Heroico*, the most reproduced photograph in history.

In *Che's Afterlife: The Legacy of an Image*, Michael Casey follows the remarkable story of Korda's image, its journey from casual snapshot to an omnipresent image, seen on everything from T-shirts to mugs, vodka labels to condoms, until it finally became a copyrighted brand.

In *Che Guevara: Revolutionary and Icon*, Trisha Ziff examines the many ways in which Alberto Korda's famous picture and the man himself have been stolen and used everywhere. Che's image has moved from heroic guerrilla fighter to being a pop celebrity, to being a symbol of radical chic. His image speaks volumes about society's ever-changing mores.

Che Guevara's Face: How a Cuban Photographer's Image Became a Cultural Icon by Danielle Smith-Llera also explores the journey made by Korda's snapshot.

Che: Images of a Revolutionary by Oscar Sola is one of the best photographic books about Che. Part biography and part photo album, it features 400 photographs, many of them never before published. It also follows Che's life from his childhood in Argentina through his journeys in Latin and Central America, and his birth as a revolutionary to his execution in Bolivia. His speeches are featured as well as writing by Fidel Castro and an elegy composed by American Beat poet, Allen Ginsberg.

Another wonderful, but more general book is *Fidel's Cuba: A Revolution in Pictures* by Cuban photographer Osvaldo Salas. The Cuban Revolution can be said to have been the most photogenic revolution in history and is captured in striking clarity in this lovely book. At 15 years old, Roberto Salas tagged along with father Osvaldo on an assignment to Cuba. They ended up in a front-row seat to the revolution. Now 78, Roberto Salas is recognized as one of the most important figures in the creation of the media image of the Cuban Revolution. The Bay of Pigs invasion, the only known meeting between Ernest Hemingway and Fidel Castro, Che Guevara, and the daily life of the Cuban people are all chronicled on the pages of this marvelous book.

For *Che: The Photobiography of Che Guevara*, Christophe Loviny was fortunate enough to have been allowed access to the Cuban photographic archives. Covering Che's entire life, the book includes numerous never-before-seen pictures as well as fascinating primary source documents.

Aleida March, Che's second wife, has played a part in a couple of photographic records of her husband's life. She wrote the introduction to the 2015 book *Che & Fidel: Images from History*, featuring a collection of fifty photographs of the architects of the Cuban Revolution, Che and Fidel.

Aleida and her children also gave support to Victor Casaus's *Self Portrait Che Guevara*, a photographic and literary memoir in which Che is presented in his own words. Unpublished short stories are included as well as his letters, poems, and photos from the Guevara family album. The hard-line revolutionary makes way for a sensitive artistic soul in this book that reveals a man of remarkable candor, irony, wit and passion.

Finally, in *The Ghosts of Ñancahuazú*, writer and artist Leandro Katz seeks out Freddy Alborta, who took the last photographs of Che after his capture and execution in Bolivia. The book includes works by Katz, Alborta's photos, as well as essays on Che by John Berger, Jean Franco, Eduardo Gruner, Mariano Mestman, and Jeffrey Skoller.

TRAVEL BOOKS

Che's journeys in Latin America have inspired many to follow in his footsteps and some have also written about their experiences.

Mauktik Kulkarni traveled thousands of miles in *A Ghost of Che: A Motorcycle Ride Through Space, Time, Life and Love*. Setting off from Louisville, Kentucky, he traveled south

into Latin America. Along the way, he muses on the human condition and finds goodness in people.

Patrick Symmes, on the other hand, jumped on his BMW R80/GS in *Chasing Che: A Motorcycle Journey in Search of the Guevara Legend* to follow the route across South America that Che took in 1952. Symmes looks for the people Che met and the places he visited. Like Che, Symmes has adventures such as running out of petrol in the Argentine desert and breaking down in the Andes. He also gets drunk with Che's traveling companion Alberto Granado.

Employing a bicycle instead of a motorbike, plucky ex-headmistress Anne Mustoe undertook a remarkable journey through South America, following in Che's tracks. In *Che Guevara and the Mountain of Silver: By Bicycle and Train through South America*, she retraces the route he took in *The Motorcycle Diaries*, providing a beautifully written chronicle of an epic journey through some of the most interesting and historically resonant places in South America.

Barbara Brodman was the first person to retrace Che's 1952 route through South America. Her 1997 book, *Looking for Mr. Guevara: A Journey through South America*, expands upon the online diaries to which thousands had access as she traveled. She describes the many adventures she had *en route*, joining an extreme rafting expedition, jumping from a sinking river boat, and rowing 375 miles in a dugout canoe.

Che and Alberto Granado's 1952 journey is also re-run in *To Infinity and Beyond: What Che Guevara Started, Somebody Had to Finish* by Stephen Holmes. He and Pete Sandford rode their authentic period Norton motorcycles through Argentina, Chile, Peru, Colombia, and Venezuela, encountering some of the most dangerous environments on the planet, including the perilous Atacama Desert in Chile, and the Amazon River. Holmes and Sandford tried to complete the journey that Che's Poderosa II never finished.

A movie poster for *Che: The Argentine* (2008) starring Benicio del Toro.

CHAPTER 20

CHE ON THE SCREEN

FILMS

Che's first fictional appearance on the silver screen did not bode well for the future. In fact, *Che!* directed by Richard Fleischer and starring Omar Sharif and Jack Palance bombed when it was released in 1969 and has since been listed in the 1978 book, *The Fifty Worst Films of All Time*. A biopic, it shows Che, played by Sharif, gaining the respect of his men during the Revolution and impressing Fidel Castro, played by Palance.

Che conducts a series of reprisals after the fall of Batista and the guerrillas' victory but his dreams of global revolution are never far from his mind. He leaves Cuba because of what he perceives as Castro's weakness during the Cuban Missile Crisis and the film ends in Bolivia. One critic said of it: "In this badly misconceived pseudo-biography of the legendary Cuban revolutionary—played, incredibly, by Omar Sharif—Che Guevara takes up the cause as a rebel fighter under the direction of Fidel Castro, played—also incredibly—by Jack Palance."

Also a difficult watch is *Utopia*, directed by

A scene from *The Motorcycle Diaries* (2004) starring Rodrigo de la Serna (left) as Alberto Granado and Gael García Bernal as Che.

James Benning in 1998. *Utopia* is a radically *avant garde* film that consists of filmmaker Robert Kramer reading Che's Bolivian diary entries. Images of buildings, roads, cars, soldiers, and others appear fleetingly on the screen. One commentator has described it as being like "found footage assembled by aliens after the end of human civilization."

In a different league altogether was Brazilian director Walter Salles' *The Motorcycle Diaries*, starring Gael García Bernal. Salles based this 2004 film on Che's book, *The Motorcycle Diaries*, the chronicle of his 1952 journey through Latin America with his friend Alberto Granado. One commentator remarked that "The Che of *The Motorcycle Diaries* is more akin to Jack Kerouac or Neal Cassady than Marx or Lenin," but it was received very positively by critics. Britain's *Daily Telegraph* said of it:

> *"The Motorcycle Diaries" may not provide any satisfactory answers as to how a 23-year-old medical student went on to become arguably the most famous revolutionary of the latter half of the 20th century, but it has an undeniable charm in that it imbues the memories of youth with a sense of altruism and purity— which are complemented by the scenery. It's an incomplete portrait to be sure, but it's a gorgeous depiction of two best friends riding unknowingly into the history books.*

Less successful was 2005's *Che Guevara*, directed by Josh Evans and starring Eduardo Noriega. A disappointing rendition of the life of Che, the film was described by one reviewer as "embarrassingly bad." Noriega, a fine actor, tries hard but he is beaten by stilted dialogue, a lack of momentum, poor editing, and little or no character development. This film does Che Guevara no favors whatsoever.

Che, directed by the hugely respected Stephen Soderbergh and starring Benicio del Toro is a two-part biopic. The films do not present Che's life in chronological order, but rather they offer a series of moments and incidents along the timeline. *Part One - The Argentine*—deals with the Cuban Revolution and the fall of the Batista regime while *Part Two - Guerrilla*—focuses on Che's attempt to export revolution to Bolivia. Shot in a *cinéma verité* style, the two films were released in 2008 and were well-received by the critics although a number described them as too long. A review in *The New York Times* said:

> *Mr. Soderbergh once again offers a master class in filmmaking. As history, though,* Che *is finally not epic but romance. It takes great care to be true to the factual record, but it is, nonetheless, a fairy tale.*

Winning the Best Actor award at the Cannes Film Festival, Benicio del Toro dedicated it to Che.

DOCUMENTARIES

There have been countless documentaries about Che's life and achievements. There is space here for only a few of them.

Eduardo Montes-Bradley's 2006 film, *Che: Rise and Fall*, was shot entirely in Cuba around the time when Che's remains were being airlifted from Bolivia to his final resting place in the specially built mausoleum at Santa Clara in Cuba. It features testimonies by the men who fought alongside the great guerrilla leader in the Sierra Maestra, the Congo, and in Bolivia. Alberto Granado, his companion on his motorbike journey of 1952, also features. Original archive footage is used as well as original photographs taken by Che in Mexico.

Also released in 2006 is *The Hands of Che Guevara*, directed by Dutchman Peter de Koch. After Che's execution in 1967, his hands were amputated for purposes of identification. This film documents de Koch's search for those severed hands which were not found with his remains in 1997.

Chevolution, directed by Luis Lopez, is a 2008 examination of the history and legacy of Alberto Korda's famous photograph of Che. The film chronicles how the photograph came to be taken and examines the many meanings and interpretations it has taken on over the decades. It also looks at its commercialization and the comparison of Che with Christ that arose after the photograph of his dead body by Freddy Alborta was released.

CHAPTER 21

CHE ON THE STAGE

PLAYS

Gay, Bangladeshi, and Italian—the range of types of play featuring Che pay testament to the width of his appeal and its global nature.

The plot of Italian playwright Mario Fratti's 1968 play, *Che Guevara*, revolves around the last part of Che's life, in particular his struggle in the jungles of Bolivia and his death at the hands of the Bolivian Army. It examines the fundamentals of organizing a revolution and champions Che's cause of a pan-continental revolution to free people from tyranny and the control of the United States. A presumed romance with Tamara Bunke Bider, "Tania the Guerrilla," also features.

The West Indian playwright Lennox Raphael's best-known work—*Che!* (1969), depicts Che as the target of sexually motivated envy by his enemies, including President John F. Kennedy, and features scenes of nudity and explicit sex. Not long after it first opened in New York City, it was closed down by New York's Public Morals Police Squad. Raphael, the actors, and the director were all arrested but the play re-opened after a judge ruled that its performance was protected by the First Amendment to the United States Constitution guaranteeing freedom of speech. In 1970, however, Raphael, the cast, the producer, and set designer were found guilty of participating in an obscene performance.

In 2001, Chinese playwright Zhang Guangtian and others wrote *Che Guevara*, a play first performed in Beijing. Described by its author as "not a biography but a reflection of the real life of a historic figure," it utilizes popular music and dance styles and the character of Che Guevara is present only through his voice and does not appear on stage.

For his 2007 play, *School of the Americas*, José Rivera, Oscar-nominated author of the screenplay for the film *The Motorcycle Diaries*, returned to the subject of Che Guevara. This time he examined the last two days of Che's life as he was held captive in the schoolhouse in La Higuera in Bolivia. He was inspired to write the play after reading a powerful interview with the Bolivian schoolteacher Julia Cortez who was with Che during those last days.

Bangladesh seems an unlikely place for someone to write a play about the great revolutionary, but Mamunur Rashid was inspired by him to write *Che'r Cycle* (2009). Written in Bengali, it begins with three characters sitting on a beach having a chat. Suddenly, these three turn into Che Guevara, Aleida March, and Fidel and Raúl Castro. The characters all interchange and move between times and places. Che's politics and attitudes help the three original characters to view life differently.

Risky Revolutionary by Fred Newman, first performed in 2010, aimed high, a historical fantasy in which Che is reunited with his revolutionary brother-in-arms, Fidel Castro, whom he persuades to stage a second Cuban Revolution. This time, however, it is a revolution that will bring human, civil, and gay rights to the people of the island.

MUSICALS

Given that Che Guevara was notoriously tone-deaf, there is a certain irony in him being associated with musicals, no matter how tenuous. The most successful is Andrew Lloyd Webber and Tim Rice's 1978 work *Evita*, although it is uncertain whether the character it features is actually Che Guevara. Even its creator, Tim Rice, seems unsure.

Both a rock opera and a film, *Evita* chronicles the life of the Argentinean political leader Eva Perón, and it won a Laurence

Olivier Award and a Tony Award for Best Musical. Rice created a character named Che to serve as narrator of the story, claiming that the character was not necessarily based on Che Guevara although there are elements that clearly could apply only to him. The film version that followed in 1996 with Madonna in the title role and Antonio Banderas as Che was nominated for five Academy Awards, winning one for Best Original Song.

A little more serious was *Che: The Argentine Musical*, by Oscar Mangione and Oscar Laiguera, first performed in 2009. This Argentine musical was an attempt, as Oscar Mangione, one of its creators, has said "to show Che not as a T-shirt icon but to get him into people's heads and hearts." They claim to try to represent the guerrilla leader seriously and honestly, and in doing so use a lot of the Latin American music styles that were around during his travels and his life.

Elaine Paige in the title role of Evita with David Essex as Che Guevara on stage in 1978, in the musical *Evita* written by Andrew Lloyd Webber and Tim Rice.

SONGS AND MUSIC

The great jazz bassist, Charlie Haden, composed *Song for Che* after he heard the news of the revolutionary's death. On stage in Portugal in 1971, he dedicated the tune to the freedom fighters in Portugal's colonies of Mozambique, Angola, and Guinea-Bissau who were trying to cast off the Portuguese yoke. The day after his performance, he was arrested, imprisoned, and interrogated for several days. His release was finally secured by the American Embassy.

Cuban musician Carlos Puebla composed the song *Hasta Siempre, Comandante* ("Until forever, Commander!") after Che left Cuba to export the Revolution. The title refers to Che's saying: "Hasta la victoria siempre!" ("Until victory, always!") and the song's lyrics are a reply to Che's farewell letter when he departed the island. They recount important moments in the Cuban Revolution and describe his role as a commander of part of the rebel force. The chorus goes:

> *We will carry on*
> *As we followed you then*
> *And with Fidel we say to you:*
> *"Until forever, Commander!"*

The song has been sung since by many artists including the Buena Vista Social Club and French singer Nathalie Cardone's modern version has sold more than 800,000 copies.

Folk singer Judy Collins has always said the ballad *Che* that she composed after his death is one of her favorite songs. James Mudriczki remixed the song for a Judy Collins tribute album *Born to the Breed*, a version that has been described as an "intense rhythmic interpretation."

Hans Werner Henze, the avant-garde German composer, described his 1968 oratorio *Das Floss der Medusa* ("The Raft of the Medusa") as a requiem for Che Guevara while Scottish songwriter, Ewan MacColl wrote *The Compañeros* in honor of Che and the Cuban Revolution. Meanwhile, Peggy Seeger, MacColl's American folk-singer wife, wrote *A Song for Che Guevara*. Even rap artist Jay-Z has got in on the act, the song *Public Service*

Announcement on his Black Album containing the lines: "I'm like Che Guevara with bling on/I'm complex." The Rolling Stones, too, mention Che in their song *Indian Girl* from their *Emotional Rescue* album. Mick Jagger intones: "Mr. Gringo, my father ain't no Che Guevara/And he's fighting the war on the streets of Masaya."

For some reason, David Bowie included the picture of Che's corpse surrounded by the Bolivian soldiers who had killed him on the inside sleeve of his album *Lodger* and Madonna imitated *Guerrillero Heroico* on the cover of her 2003 *American Life* album, describing Che as a "revolutionary spirit." Rage Against the Machine sell merchandise with Che's image and in the liner notes to one of their albums, they even recommend Che's book *Guerrilla Warfare*.

Che's name crops up in songs by a variety of artists including The Pet Shop Boys (*Left to My Own Devices*) and The Manic Street Preachers (*Revol*).

There has even been an opera about Che—the 1969 work, *Reconstructie. Een moraliteit* ("Reconstruction. A Morality"). A collaborative composition, it featured the work of Dutch and Belgian composers Reinbert de Leeuw, Harry Mulisch, Peter Schat, Hugo Claus, Louis Andriessen, and Misha Mengelberg and was inspired by Mozart's *Don Giovanni*. The opera takes place mainly during the time Che was in Bolivia.

GAMING

Cuba and Che have featured in a number of games over the years, the revolutionary's image being purloined on a regular basis.

The 1987 video game *Guevara*, released by SNK in Japan, was re-named *Guerrilla War* when published in the West. It featured Che and his exploits during the Cuban Revolution, but when released in the West all references to him were removed. The game map, however, still closely resembles the island of Cuba. The original Japanese *Guevara* edition of this game sells for large sums to collectors due to its rarity.

Tropico is a 2001 construction and management simulation video game, a game genre whose early success was generated by games such as *Sim City*. In *Tropico*, players have the opportunity to govern a tropical island which resembles Cuba after the Revolution. They can elect to design their own "El Presidente" character or may choose from a list of already created historical figures, one of which is Che Guevara.

The Revolution also features in the 2009 cellphone game *El Che*, released by GlobalFun who described it as "great looking, action packed, freedom fighting excursion into the historical battles of Sierra Maestra, Bueycito and Santa Clara." Rather disturbingly, the player gets to choose from an arsenal of assault rifles, grenades, and rocket launchers in order to "bring peace to impoverished Cuba."

In the Playstation action-adventure stealth video game *Metal Gear Solid: Peace Walker*, published by Konami, the "Big Boss" character resembles Che both in appearance and in ideology. Other characters in the game point out the resemblance and Che's name is mentioned several times during the game's audio briefings.

Needless to say, the famous photograph of Che—*Guerrillero Heroico*—pops up in games. Jim Fitzpatrick's version of the picture appears in the first-person shooter video game *Call of Duty: Black Ops*. One of the multi-player maps to be played is called "Havana" and Che's image appears on the wall among other works of art.

The box art for the action-adventure video game *Just Cause* imitates Alberto Korda's famous photo. Furthermore, the game's hero is Rico Rodriguez who is based on Félix Rodríguez, the CIA agent who was in La Higuera when Che was executed.

The image appeared again when a new world record for toppling dominoes was established in 2008. For two hours, 4,345,027 dominoes fell over to reveal, along with other images, a portrait of Che Guevara.

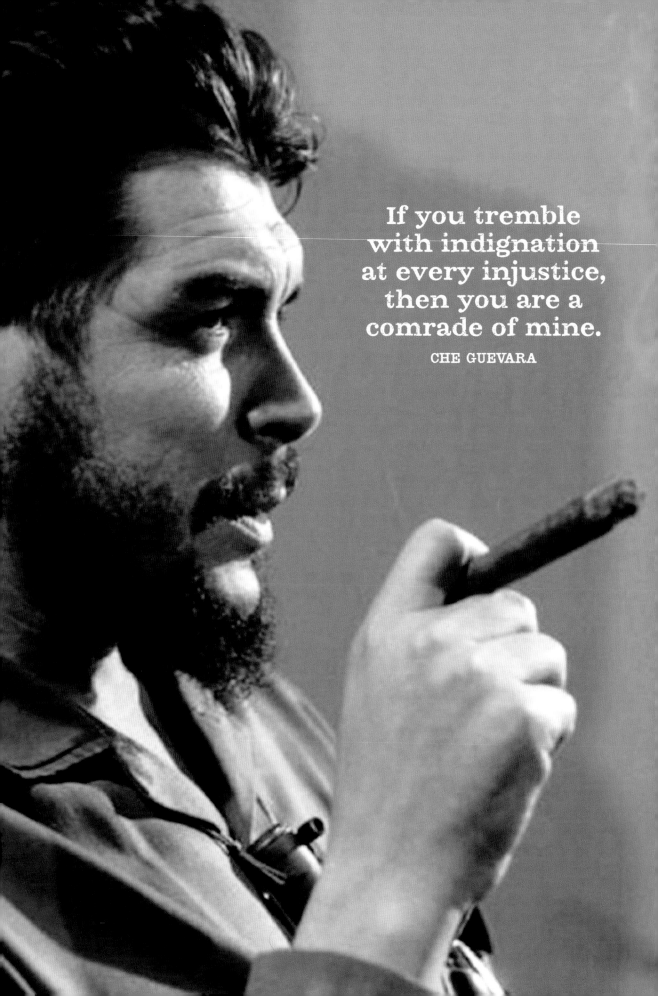

If you tremble
with indignation
at every injustice,
then you are a
comrade of mine.

CHE GUEVARA

FURTHER READING

This book documents the life and times of Che Guevara and is designed to be an informative and entertaining introductory text. There are many more academic publications available should the reader wish to delve more deeply. Publications that were especially useful during the preparation of this book are listed below, and other credits are cited at the point where they appear within the text.

Alvarez de Toledo, Lucia, *The Story of Che Guevara*. London, Quercus, 2011.

Anderson, Jon Lee, *Che Guevara: A Revolutionary Life*. London, Bantam Press, 1997.

Bustos, Ciro, *Che Wants to See You: The Untold Story of Che*. London, Verso, 2013.

Castañeda, Jorge G., *Compañero: The Life and Death of Che Guevara*. London, Bloomsbury, 1997.

Castro, Fidel, *Che: A Memoir by Fidel Castro*. Melbourne, Australia, Ocean Press, 1994.

Debray, Régis, *La Guerrilla de Che*. Paris, Maspéro, 1974.

Gadea, Hilda, *Ernesto: A Memoir of Che Guevara: An Intimate Account of the Making of a Revolutionary by His First Wife, Hilda Gadea*. London, W.H. Allen, 1973.

Gadea, Hilda, *My Life With Che: The Making of a Revolutionary*. New York, St. Martin's Press, 2009.

Granado, Alberto, *Traveling with Che Guevara: The Making of a Revolutionary*. London, Pimlico, 2003.

Guevara, Ernesto Che, *Bolivian Diary*. Trans. Carlos P. Hansen and Andrew Sinclair. London, Jonathan Cape/Lorrimer, 1968.

Guevara, Ernesto Che, *Episodes of the Cuban Revolutionary War*. New York, Pathfinder, 1996.

Guevara, Ernesto Che, *Guerrilla Warfare*. Lincoln and London, University of Nebraska Press, 1985.

Guevara, Ernesto Che, *The Motorcycle Diaries: Notes on a Latin American Diary*. London, Verso, 1994.

Guevara, Ernesto Che, *Venceremos!: The Speeches and Writings of Ernesto Che Guevara*. Ed. John Gerassi. London, Weidenfeld & Nicolson, 1968.

Guevara, Ernesto Che & Castro, Fidel, *Socialism and Man in Cuba*. New York, Pathfinder, 2009.

Guevara Lynch, Ernesto, *The Young Che: Memories of Che Guevara*. London, Vintage, 2007.

James, Daniel, *Che Guevara: A Biography*. New York, Stein and Day, 1969.

March, Aleida, *Remembering Che: My Life with Che Guevara*. Melbourne, Australia, Ocean Press, 2008.

Reid-Henry, Simon, *Fidel and Che: A Revolutionary Friendship*. London, Hodder & Stoughton, 2009.

Rojo, Ricardo, *My Friend Che*. New York, Dial Press, 1968.

Sinclair, Andrew, *Che Guevara*. London, Fontana/Collins, 1979.

Villegas, Harry (Pombo), *Pombo: A Man of Che's Guerrilla: With Che Guevara in Bolivia 1966-68*. Atlanta, Pathfinder Books, 1997.

A bronze statue of Che designed by sculptor José Delarra stands outside the Communist Party headquarters in Santa Clara, Cuba.

INDEX

Note: Page numbers in *italic* refer to photographs

Inspiring | Educating | Creating | Entertaining

Brimming with creative inspiration, how-to projects, and useful information to enrich your everyday life, Quarto Knows is a favorite destination for those pursuing their interests and passions. Visit our site and dig deeper with our books into your area of interest: Quarto Creates, Quarto Cooks, Quarto Homes, Quarto Lives, Quarto Drives, Quarto Explores, Quarto Gifts, or Quarto Kids.

Picture Credits

The images listed below are in the public domain (PD) unless otherwise stated. Kind thanks to Museo Ernesto Che Guevara (MECG) in Alta Gracia, Cordoba, Argentina and the Centro de Estudios Che Guevara (CDECG) in Havana, Cuba for some of the photographs. Interested readers can visit their websites for further information: www.welcomeargentina.com/altagracia/ernesto-che-guevara-museum; www.ecured.cu/Centro_de_Estudios_Che_Guevara.

Cover images: Alberto Korda 1960; *Verde Oliva* 1959; Bettmann Getty; PD MECG.

Internal images: 2 PD Alberto Korda 1960 / 4 PD MECG / 6 Michael Nicholson/Corbis/Getty / 7 Hulton Archive/Getty / 8 PD MECG / 10 Apic/Getty / 10 PD MECG / 11 PD MECG /13 Bettmann Getty / 14 Apic/Getty / 15 Prisma by Dukas Presseagentur GmbH/Alamy / 16 PD portal.educ.ar / 18 PD / 22 Apic/Getty/ 23 Emiliano Rodriguez/Alamy / 24 PD CDECG / 25 PD CDECG / 26 John van Hasselt/Sygma/Getty Images / 28 Entertainment Pictures/Alamy / 30 *Verde Oliva* 1959 / 32 Gilberto Ante/Roger Viollet/Getty / 33 PD MECG / 35 Jose Goitia/Gamma-Rapho/Getty / 36 © Yousuf Karsh 1971 / 38 Hulton-Deutsch/Corbis/Getty / 39 Bettmann Getty / 41 M. Stroud/Daily Express/Hulton Archive/Getty / 42 George Silk/The Life Picture Collection/Getty / 43 Frank Scherschel/The Life Picture Collection/Getty / 45 Lester Cole/Corbis/Getty / 46 Bettmann Getty / 47 Keystone-France/Gamma-Keystone/Getty / 48 Thomas D. Mcavoy/The Life Picture Collection/Getty / 50 Bettmann Getty / 52 Santi Burgos/Bloomberg/Getty / 52 PD MECG / 53 *La Habana Literaria* 1892 / 55 Bettmann Getty / 56 Keystone-France/Gamma-Keystone/Getty / 57 Torontonian/Alamy / 58 Photo12/UIG/Getty / 59 Ullstein bild/Getty / 60 Photo12/UIG/Getty / 61 AFP/Getty / 62 Pictorial Parade/Archive Photos/Getty / 63 Alain Nogues/Sygma/Getty / 64 Alain Nogues/Sygma/Getty / 66 PD CDECG / 68 Salas Archive Photos/Alamy / 69 Bettmann/Getty / 70 Sean Pavone/Alamy / 71 Rolls Press/Popperfoto/Getty / 72 AFP/Getty / 74 Joseph Scherschel/The Life Picture Collection/Getty / 75 World History Archive/Alamy / 77 Pool Loviny Korda/Gamma-Rapho/Getty / 78 PD Alberto Korda 1960 / 81 TASS/Getty / 82 Gilberto Ante/Roger Viollet/Getty / 81 Bertrand Rindoff Petroff/Getty / 82 Johannes Jansson / 83 World History Archive/Alamy / 84 Bettmann Getty / 85 Allan Seiden, Legacy Archive/Getty / 86 PD / 87 Salas Archive Photos/Alamy / 88 PD CDECG/Alberto Korda / 90 Itar-Tass/Alamy / 91 PD US Federal Government/US Air Force/CIA / Johner Images/Alamy / 92 Corbis/Getty / 93 a26invader@outlook.com / 94 Keystone-France/Gamma-Keystone/Getty / 95 Bettmann Getty / 96 Bettmann/Getty / 97 Bettmann/Getty / 98 PD USgov / 99 Deutsches Bundesarchiv 1963 /100 Bettmann/Getty / 101 World History Archive/Alamy / 103 Fine Art Images/Heritage Images/Getty / 104 Corbis/Getty / 105 Stan Wayman/The Life Picture Collection/Getty / 106 ABC/Getty / 108 Keystone-France/Gamma-Keystone/Getty / 110 www.museuvirtualcheguevara.com / 111 www.polemicacubana.fr / 113 Bettmann Getty / 114 Sven Creutzmann/Mambo photo/Getty / 115 Don Carl Steffen/Gamma-Rapho/Getty 116 Bettmann/Getty / 118 Salas Archive Photos/Alamy / 120 Philipp Kester/ullstein bild/Getty / 123 Hulton Archive/Getty / 124 Hulton-Deutsch Collection/Corbis/Getty / 126 PD *Prensa Latina* 1959 / 128 Tass/Getty / 130 Horst Zimmermann/ullstein bild/Getty / 132 Hulton Archive/Getty / 133 PD Private Collection / 134 Keystone-France/Gamma-Keystone/Getty/ 135 AFP/Getty / 136 World History Archive/Alamy / 138 CBS Photo Archive/Getty / 141 Keystone-France/Gamma-Keystone/Getty / 143 Emiliano Rodriguez/Alamy / 144 AFP/Getty / 147 AFP/Getty / 149 Bettmann Getty / 151 Paul Slade/Paris Match/Getty / 152 Keystone-France/Gamma-Keystone/Getty / 154 Joseph Fabry/The Life Images Collection/Getty / 156 Bettmann Getty / 158 Bettmann Getty/ Nemanja Otic/ Alamy / 159 Paul Slade/Paris Match/Getty / 160 Hulton Archive/Getty / 162 PD/ 163 Brian Moser/Eye Ubiquitous/Corbis/Getty / 164 Marc Hutten/AFP/Getty 165 Keystone-France/Gamma-Keystone/Getty / 166 Freddy Alborta/Bride Lane Library/Popperfoto/Getty / 168 Claude Urraca/Sygma/Getty / 170 Adalberto Roque/AFP/Getty / 172 Sven Creutzmann/Mambo Photography/Getty / 173 Sven Creutzmann/Mambo Photography/Getty / 174 Federico Scoppa/AFP/Getty / 176 Urbano Delvalle/The Life Images Collection/Getty / 178 www.versobooks.com / 180 www.impawards.com / 181 Everett Collection Inc / Alamy / 184 Central Press/Getty / 186 © Elliott Erwitt 1964 / 188 Roberto Machado Noa/LightRocket/Getty.